50 Greek Pizza Recipes for Home

By: Kelly Johnson

Table of Contents

- Classic Greek Margherita Pizza
- Greek Salad Pizza with Feta and Olives
- Spinach and Feta Pita Pizza
- Mediterranean Veggie Pizza
- Greek Chicken Souvlaki Pizza
- Tzatziki and Hummus Pita Pizza
- Lamb and Mint Greek Pizza
- Artichoke and Kalamata Olive Pizza
- Greek-Style BBQ Chicken Pizza
- Greek Gyro Pizza with Tzatziki Sauce
- Tomato and Olive Fougasse Pizza
- Spanakopita-Inspired Pizza
- Greek Flatbread Pizza with Sun-Dried Tomatoes
- Lemon and Oregano Chicken Pita Pizza
- Mediterranean Seafood Pizza
- Roasted Red Pepper and Feta Pizza
- Grilled Zucchini and Halloumi Pizza
- Greek Eggplant and Tomato Pizza
- Hummus and Roasted Vegetable Pita Pizza
- Greek Shrimp Scampi Pizza
- Greek-Style Lamb Meatball Pizza
- Chickpea and Feta Pita Pizza
- Mediterranean Pesto Pizza
- Greek Chicken and Olive Naan Pizza
- Spinach and Feta Stuffed Crust Pizza
- Mediterranean Fig and Prosciutto Pizza
- Greek Bruschetta Pizza
- Mediterranean Turkey and Spinach Pizza
- Greek Spanakopita Pizza Rolls
- Quinoa and Olive Greek Pizza
- Greek Moussaka Pizza
- Grilled Greek Pizza Skewers
- Mediterranean Tuna and Red Onion Pizza
- Greek Orzo Salad Pizza
- Pita Bread Breakfast Pizza with Greek Yogurt

- Fennel and Artichoke Greek Pizza
- Greek-inspired Pita Calzone
- Tomato and Olive Pesto Pita Pizza
- Greek Tandoori Chicken Pizza
- Greek Hummus and Pita Pizza
- Mediterranean Roasted Vegetable Flatbread Pizza
- Greek Potato and Rosemary Pizza
- Smoked Salmon and Cream Cheese Greek Pizza
- Spinach and Olive Greek Pizza Breadsticks
- Greek Fava Bean and Mint Pizza
- Greek Avocado and Tomato Pizza
- Mediterranean Quiche Pizza
- Greek Feta and Honey Pizza
- Kalamata Olive and Rosemary Focaccia Pizza
- Grilled Greek Pizza Panini

Classic Greek Margherita Pizza

Ingredients:

For the Dough:

- 1 pound pizza dough (homemade or store-bought)

For the Toppings:

- 1 cup tomato sauce or crushed tomatoes
- 1 1/2 cups fresh mozzarella, sliced
- 1 cup cherry tomatoes, halved
- 1/2 cup Kalamata olives, sliced
- 1/4 cup crumbled feta cheese
- Fresh basil leaves, for garnish
- Extra virgin olive oil, for drizzling
- Salt and black pepper to taste

Instructions:

Preheat the Oven:
- Preheat your oven to the highest temperature it can go (usually around 475-500°F or 245-260°C).

Prepare the Dough:
- If using store-bought dough, follow the package instructions for bringing it to room temperature. If making homemade dough, roll it out on a floured surface to your desired thickness.

Assemble the Pizza:
- Place the rolled-out dough on a pizza stone or a baking sheet.
- Spread the tomato sauce evenly over the dough, leaving a border around the edges for the crust.
- Arrange the sliced fresh mozzarella, halved cherry tomatoes, and Kalamata olives on top of the sauce.
- Sprinkle crumbled feta cheese over the pizza.

Bake the Pizza:
- Place the pizza in the preheated oven and bake for 12-15 minutes or until the crust is golden and the cheese is melted and bubbly.

Finish and Garnish:

- Remove the pizza from the oven. Sprinkle fresh basil leaves over the hot pizza.
- Drizzle extra virgin olive oil over the pizza and season with salt and black pepper to taste.

Slice and Serve:
- Allow the pizza to cool for a few minutes before slicing. Serve and enjoy your Greek-inspired Margherita pizza!

This fusion pizza combines the classic Margherita elements with Greek flavors, creating a delicious and unique culinary experience.

Greek Salad Pizza with Feta and Olives

Ingredients:

For the Pizza Dough:

- 1 pound pizza dough (homemade or store-bought)

For the Toppings:

- 1/2 cup hummus (used as the pizza sauce)
- 1 cup cherry tomatoes, halved
- 1/2 cucumber, thinly sliced
- 1/4 red onion, thinly sliced
- 1/2 cup Kalamata olives, sliced
- 1 cup crumbled feta cheese
- Fresh oregano leaves (or dried oregano)
- Extra virgin olive oil, for drizzling
- Salt and black pepper to taste

Instructions:

Preheat the Oven:
- Preheat your oven to the highest temperature it can go (usually around 475-500°F or 245-260°C).

Prepare the Dough:
- If using store-bought dough, follow the package instructions for bringing it to room temperature. If making homemade dough, roll it out on a floured surface to your desired thickness.

Assemble the Pizza:
- Place the rolled-out dough on a pizza stone or a baking sheet.
- Spread hummus evenly over the dough, leaving a border around the edges for the crust.
- Arrange halved cherry tomatoes, sliced cucumber, and red onion over the hummus.
- Sprinkle Kalamata olives and crumbled feta cheese evenly over the pizza.

Bake the Pizza:

- Place the pizza in the preheated oven and bake for 12-15 minutes or until the crust is golden and the toppings are heated through.

Finish and Garnish:
- Remove the pizza from the oven. Sprinkle fresh oregano leaves (or dried oregano) over the hot pizza.
- Drizzle extra virgin olive oil over the pizza and season with salt and black pepper to taste.

Slice and Serve:
- Allow the pizza to cool for a few minutes before slicing. Serve and enjoy your Greek Salad Pizza with Feta and Olives!

This pizza combines the freshness of a Greek salad with the rich flavors of feta and olives, creating a delicious and Mediterranean-inspired meal. Feel free to customize the toppings based on your preferences.

Spinach and Feta Pita Pizza

Ingredients:

- 4 whole wheat pita bread rounds
- 1 cup fresh spinach leaves, washed and chopped
- 1 cup crumbled feta cheese
- 1 cup cherry tomatoes, halved
- 1/4 cup red onion, thinly sliced
- 2 cloves garlic, minced
- 2 tablespoons olive oil
- 1 teaspoon dried oregano
- Salt and black pepper to taste
- Optional: Kalamata olives, sliced, for extra flavor

Instructions:

Preheat the Oven:
- Preheat your oven to 375°F (190°C).

Prepare Pita Bread:
- Place the pita bread rounds on a baking sheet.

Prepare Spinach and Feta Topping:
- In a bowl, mix together chopped spinach, crumbled feta cheese, cherry tomatoes, sliced red onion, minced garlic, and optional sliced Kalamata olives.

Assemble Pita Pizzas:
- Spoon the spinach and feta topping mixture evenly over each pita bread round.

Drizzle with Olive Oil:
- Drizzle olive oil over the toppings on each pita.

Season and Sprinkle Oregano:
- Season with salt and black pepper to taste. Sprinkle dried oregano over the pizzas.

Bake:
- Place the baking sheet in the preheated oven and bake for 10-12 minutes or until the edges of the pita are golden and the toppings are heated through.

Finish and Serve:
- Remove the pita pizzas from the oven and let them cool for a few minutes.

- Optionally, you can sprinkle a bit more feta, oregano, or fresh herbs over the top before serving.

Slice and Enjoy:
- Slice the Spinach and Feta Pita Pizzas into wedges and serve. Enjoy your quick and flavorful Mediterranean-inspired meal!

This Spinach and Feta Pita Pizza is not only easy to make but also a delicious and nutritious option for a light lunch or dinner. The combination of spinach and feta creates a classic Mediterranean flavor that's both satisfying and wholesome.

Mediterranean Veggie Pizza

Ingredients:

For the Pizza Dough:

- 1 pound pizza dough (homemade or store-bought)

For the Toppings:

- 1/2 cup hummus (used as the pizza sauce)
- 1 cup cherry tomatoes, halved
- 1/2 cucumber, thinly sliced
- 1/4 red onion, thinly sliced
- 1/2 cup Kalamata olives, sliced
- 1/2 cup crumbled feta cheese
- 1/4 cup fresh basil leaves, chopped
- 2 tablespoons extra virgin olive oil
- 1 teaspoon dried oregano
- Salt and black pepper to taste

Instructions:

Preheat the Oven:
- Preheat your oven to the highest temperature it can go (usually around 475-500°F or 245-260°C).

Prepare the Dough:
- If using store-bought dough, follow the package instructions for bringing it to room temperature. If making homemade dough, roll it out on a floured surface to your desired thickness.

Assemble the Pizza:
- Place the rolled-out dough on a pizza stone or a baking sheet.
- Spread hummus evenly over the dough, leaving a border around the edges for the crust.
- Arrange halved cherry tomatoes, thinly sliced cucumber, and red onion over the hummus.
- Scatter sliced Kalamata olives and crumbled feta cheese evenly over the pizza.
- Sprinkle fresh basil leaves over the toppings.

Drizzle with Olive Oil:
- Drizzle extra virgin olive oil over the pizza.

Season and Sprinkle Oregano:
- Season with dried oregano, salt, and black pepper to taste.

Bake the Pizza:
- Place the pizza in the preheated oven and bake for 12-15 minutes or until the crust is golden and the toppings are heated through.

Finish and Serve:
- Remove the pizza from the oven. Allow it to cool for a few minutes.

Slice and Enjoy:
- Slice the Mediterranean Veggie Pizza into wedges and serve. Enjoy your flavorful and healthy pizza inspired by the Mediterranean cuisine!

This pizza showcases the vibrant flavors of the Mediterranean with a combination of fresh vegetables, olives, and feta cheese. It's a delightful and nutritious option for those who enjoy the rich and diverse tastes of Mediterranean cuisine.

Greek Chicken Souvlaki Pizza

Ingredients:

For the Chicken Souvlaki:

- 1 pound boneless, skinless chicken breasts, cut into bite-sized pieces
- 3 tablespoons olive oil
- 2 tablespoons Greek yogurt
- 2 tablespoons lemon juice
- 2 teaspoons dried oregano
- 2 teaspoons minced garlic
- Salt and black pepper to taste
- Wooden skewers (pre-soaked in water)

For the Pizza:

- 1 pound pizza dough (homemade or store-bought)
- 1/2 cup Tzatziki sauce (store-bought or homemade)
- 1 cup cherry tomatoes, halved
- 1/2 cucumber, thinly sliced
- 1/4 red onion, thinly sliced
- 1/2 cup Kalamata olives, sliced
- 1 cup crumbled feta cheese
- Fresh oregano leaves for garnish
- Extra virgin olive oil for drizzling

Instructions:

For the Chicken Souvlaki:

Marinate the Chicken:
- In a bowl, whisk together olive oil, Greek yogurt, lemon juice, dried oregano, minced garlic, salt, and black pepper.
- Add the chicken pieces to the marinade, ensuring they are well coated. Marinate for at least 30 minutes, or refrigerate for a few hours for enhanced flavor.

Skewer the Chicken:
- Thread the marinated chicken pieces onto the pre-soaked wooden skewers.

Grill the Chicken:
- Preheat a grill or grill pan over medium-high heat. Grill the chicken skewers for 6-8 minutes, turning occasionally, until fully cooked and slightly charred. Remove from the grill and set aside.

For the Pizza:

Preheat the Oven:
- Preheat your oven to the highest temperature it can go (usually around 475-500°F or 245-260°C).

Prepare the Dough:
- If using store-bought dough, follow the package instructions for bringing it to room temperature. If making homemade dough, roll it out on a floured surface to your desired thickness.

Assemble the Pizza:
- Place the rolled-out dough on a pizza stone or a baking sheet.
- Spread Tzatziki sauce evenly over the dough, leaving a border around the edges for the crust.
- Distribute the grilled chicken evenly over the Tzatziki-covered dough.
- Arrange halved cherry tomatoes, thinly sliced cucumber, sliced red onion, and Kalamata olives over the pizza.
- Scatter crumbled feta cheese over the toppings.

Bake the Pizza:
- Place the pizza in the preheated oven and bake for 12-15 minutes or until the crust is golden and the toppings are heated through.

Finish and Serve:
- Remove the pizza from the oven. Drizzle extra virgin olive oil over the top and garnish with fresh oregano leaves.

Slice and Enjoy:
- Slice the Greek Chicken Souvlaki Pizza into wedges and serve. Enjoy the Greek-inspired flavors in pizza form!

This pizza combines the classic Greek flavors of souvlaki with the convenience of a pizza. It's a delicious and satisfying meal that captures the essence of Greek cuisine.

Tzatziki and Hummus Pita Pizza

Ingredients:

For the Pita Pizza:

- 4 whole wheat pita bread rounds
- 1 cup hummus (store-bought or homemade)
- 1 cup tzatziki sauce (store-bought or homemade)
- 1 cup cherry tomatoes, halved
- 1/2 cucumber, thinly sliced
- 1/4 red onion, thinly sliced
- 1/2 cup Kalamata olives, sliced
- 1/2 cup crumbled feta cheese
- Fresh dill or parsley for garnish
- Extra virgin olive oil for drizzling
- Salt and black pepper to taste

Instructions:

Preheat the Oven:
- Preheat your oven to 375°F (190°C).

Prepare the Pita Bread:
- Place the whole wheat pita rounds on a baking sheet.

Assemble the Pita Pizzas:
- Spread a generous layer of hummus over each pita round, leaving a border around the edges for the crust.
- Spoon tzatziki sauce over the hummus layer on each pita.
- Arrange halved cherry tomatoes, thinly sliced cucumber, sliced red onion, and Kalamata olives over the pita pizzas.
- Scatter crumbled feta cheese evenly over the toppings.

Drizzle with Olive Oil:
- Drizzle extra virgin olive oil over the pita pizzas.

Season with Salt and Pepper:
- Season with salt and black pepper to taste.

Bake the Pita Pizzas:
- Place the baking sheet in the preheated oven and bake for 10-12 minutes or until the edges of the pita are golden, and the toppings are heated through.

Finish and Garnish:
- Remove the pita pizzas from the oven. Sprinkle fresh dill or parsley over the hot pizzas.

Slice and Serve:
- Allow the Tzatziki and Hummus Pita Pizzas to cool for a few minutes before slicing. Serve and enjoy your flavorful Mediterranean-inspired pita pizzas!

These pita pizzas are not only quick and easy to make but also full of fresh Mediterranean flavors. The combination of hummus, tzatziki, and a variety of veggies creates a delightful and satisfying meal.

Lamb and Mint Greek Pizza

Ingredients:

For the Lamb:

- 1 pound ground lamb
- 1 tablespoon olive oil
- 1 small onion, finely chopped
- 2 cloves garlic, minced
- 1 teaspoon dried oregano
- Salt and black pepper to taste
- 1/4 cup fresh mint leaves, chopped

For the Pizza:

- 1 pound pizza dough (homemade or store-bought)
- 1/2 cup Tzatziki sauce (store-bought or homemade)
- 1 cup crumbled feta cheese
- 1 cup cherry tomatoes, halved
- 1/2 red onion, thinly sliced
- 1/4 cup Kalamata olives, sliced
- Fresh mint leaves for garnish
- Extra virgin olive oil for drizzling

Instructions:

For the Lamb:

Cook the Lamb:
- In a skillet, heat olive oil over medium heat. Add finely chopped onion and minced garlic. Sauté until softened.
- Add ground lamb to the skillet. Cook until browned and cooked through, breaking it apart with a spoon.
- Season the lamb with dried oregano, salt, and black pepper. Stir in fresh mint leaves. Cook for an additional 2-3 minutes. Remove from heat and set aside.

For the Pizza:

Preheat the Oven:
- Preheat your oven to the highest temperature it can go (usually around 475-500°F or 245-260°C).

Prepare the Dough:
- If using store-bought dough, follow the package instructions for bringing it to room temperature. If making homemade dough, roll it out on a floured surface to your desired thickness.

Assemble the Pizza:
- Place the rolled-out dough on a pizza stone or a baking sheet.
- Spread a layer of Tzatziki sauce evenly over the dough, leaving a border around the edges for the crust.
- Distribute the cooked lamb evenly over the Tzatziki-covered dough.
- Sprinkle crumbled feta cheese over the lamb.
- Arrange halved cherry tomatoes, thinly sliced red onion, and sliced Kalamata olives over the pizza.

Bake the Pizza:
- Place the pizza in the preheated oven and bake for 12-15 minutes or until the crust is golden and the toppings are heated through.

Finish and Garnish:
- Remove the pizza from the oven. Sprinkle fresh mint leaves over the hot pizza.
- Drizzle extra virgin olive oil over the pizza.

Slice and Serve:
- Allow the Lamb and Mint Greek Pizza to cool for a few minutes before slicing. Serve and enjoy this flavorful and unique pizza!

This pizza captures the essence of Greek cuisine with the savory flavors of lamb, the freshness of mint, and the classic Mediterranean toppings. It's a delicious twist on traditional pizza!

Artichoke and Kalamata Olive Pizza

Ingredients:

For the Pizza Dough:

- 1 pound pizza dough (homemade or store-bought)

For the Toppings:

- 1/2 cup pizza sauce or marinara sauce
- 1 1/2 cups shredded mozzarella cheese
- 1/2 cup grated Parmesan cheese
- 1 cup marinated artichoke hearts, drained and quartered
- 1/2 cup Kalamata olives, sliced
- 1/4 cup red onion, thinly sliced
- 2 cloves garlic, minced
- 1 teaspoon dried oregano
- Crushed red pepper flakes (optional, for a bit of heat)
- Fresh basil leaves for garnish
- Olive oil for drizzling

Instructions:

Preheat the Oven:
- Preheat your oven to the highest temperature it can go (usually around 475-500°F or 245-260°C).

Prepare the Dough:
- If using store-bought dough, follow the package instructions for bringing it to room temperature. If making homemade dough, roll it out on a floured surface to your desired thickness.

Assemble the Pizza:
- Place the rolled-out dough on a pizza stone or a baking sheet.
- Spread pizza sauce evenly over the dough, leaving a border around the edges for the crust.
- Sprinkle shredded mozzarella cheese and grated Parmesan cheese over the sauce.
- Distribute quartered marinated artichoke hearts, sliced Kalamata olives, and thinly sliced red onion over the cheese.

- Sprinkle minced garlic and dried oregano over the toppings. Add crushed red pepper flakes if you like a bit of heat.

Bake the Pizza:
- Place the pizza in the preheated oven and bake for 12-15 minutes or until the crust is golden, and the cheese is melted and bubbly.

Finish and Garnish:
- Remove the pizza from the oven. Drizzle a bit of olive oil over the hot pizza.
- Garnish with fresh basil leaves for a burst of flavor.

Slice and Serve:
- Allow the Artichoke and Kalamata Olive Pizza to cool for a few minutes before slicing. Serve and enjoy this flavorful and Mediterranean-inspired pizza!

This pizza combines the earthy flavor of artichokes, the brininess of Kalamata olives, and the richness of Parmesan for a delicious and satisfying meal.

Greek-Style BBQ Chicken Pizza

Ingredients:

For the BBQ Chicken:

- 1 pound boneless, skinless chicken breasts
- 1/2 cup Greek yogurt
- 1/4 cup olive oil
- 3 cloves garlic, minced
- 1 teaspoon dried oregano
- 1 teaspoon smoked paprika
- Salt and black pepper to taste
- 1/4 cup fresh parsley, chopped (for garnish)

For the Pizza:

- 1 pound pizza dough (homemade or store-bought)
- 1/2 cup barbecue sauce
- 1 1/2 cups shredded mozzarella cheese
- 1/2 cup crumbled feta cheese
- 1/4 cup red onion, thinly sliced
- 1/4 cup Kalamata olives, sliced
- 1/4 cup cherry tomatoes, halved
- Fresh oregano leaves for garnish
- Olive oil for drizzling

Instructions:

For the BBQ Chicken:

Marinate the Chicken:
- In a bowl, whisk together Greek yogurt, olive oil, minced garlic, dried oregano, smoked paprika, salt, and black pepper.
- Add the chicken breasts to the marinade, ensuring they are well coated. Marinate for at least 30 minutes, or refrigerate for a few hours for enhanced flavor.

Cook the Chicken:

- Preheat your grill or grill pan over medium-high heat. Grill the marinated chicken breasts for 6-8 minutes per side or until fully cooked. Allow the chicken to rest for a few minutes before slicing into thin strips.

For the Pizza:

Preheat the Oven:
- Preheat your oven to the highest temperature it can go (usually around 475-500°F or 245-260°C).

Prepare the Dough:
- If using store-bought dough, follow the package instructions for bringing it to room temperature. If making homemade dough, roll it out on a floured surface to your desired thickness.

Assemble the Pizza:
- Place the rolled-out dough on a pizza stone or a baking sheet.
- Spread barbecue sauce evenly over the dough, leaving a border around the edges for the crust.
- Sprinkle shredded mozzarella cheese over the barbecue sauce.
- Arrange sliced BBQ chicken evenly over the cheese.
- Scatter crumbled feta cheese, thinly sliced red onion, sliced Kalamata olives, and halved cherry tomatoes over the pizza.

Bake the Pizza:
- Place the pizza in the preheated oven and bake for 12-15 minutes or until the crust is golden and the cheese is melted and bubbly.

Finish and Garnish:
- Remove the pizza from the oven. Drizzle a bit of olive oil over the hot pizza.
- Garnish with fresh oregano leaves and chopped parsley.

Slice and Serve:
- Allow the Greek-Style BBQ Chicken Pizza to cool for a few minutes before slicing. Serve and enjoy this flavorful and unique pizza!

This pizza combines the smoky flavors of BBQ chicken with the richness of feta and the freshness of Greek-inspired toppings. It's a delicious fusion of barbecue and Mediterranean cuisine!

Greek Gyro Pizza with Tzatziki Sauce

Ingredients:

For the Pizza Dough:

- 1 pound pizza dough (homemade or store-bought)

For the Gyro Chicken:

- 1 pound boneless, skinless chicken breasts, thinly sliced
- 2 tablespoons olive oil
- 1 tablespoon Greek seasoning blend
- 1 teaspoon minced garlic
- Juice of 1 lemon
- Salt and black pepper to taste

For the Tzatziki Sauce:

- 1 cup Greek yogurt
- 1/2 cucumber, finely grated and drained
- 2 cloves garlic, minced
- 1 tablespoon fresh dill, chopped
- 1 tablespoon lemon juice
- Salt and black pepper to taste

For the Pizza:

- 1 cup crumbled feta cheese
- 1 cup cherry tomatoes, halved
- 1/2 red onion, thinly sliced
- 1/4 cup Kalamata olives, sliced
- Fresh oregano leaves for garnish
- Extra virgin olive oil for drizzling

Instructions:

For the Gyro Chicken:

Marinate the Chicken:
- In a bowl, combine olive oil, Greek seasoning, minced garlic, lemon juice, salt, and black pepper.
- Add thinly sliced chicken to the marinade, ensuring it's well coated. Marinate for at least 30 minutes.

Cook the Chicken:
- Heat a skillet over medium-high heat. Cook the marinated chicken slices until fully cooked and slightly caramelized. Set aside.

For the Tzatziki Sauce:

Prepare Tzatziki:
- In a bowl, combine Greek yogurt, grated cucumber, minced garlic, chopped fresh dill, lemon juice, salt, and black pepper. Mix well. Refrigerate until ready to use.

For the Pizza:

Preheat the Oven:
- Preheat your oven to the highest temperature it can go (usually around 475-500°F or 245-260°C).

Prepare the Dough:
- If using store-bought dough, follow the package instructions for bringing it to room temperature. If making homemade dough, roll it out on a floured surface to your desired thickness.

Assemble the Pizza:
- Place the rolled-out dough on a pizza stone or a baking sheet.
- Spread a layer of Tzatziki sauce evenly over the dough, leaving a border around the edges for the crust.
- Sprinkle crumbled feta cheese over the Tzatziki-covered dough.
- Distribute the cooked gyro chicken evenly over the pizza.
- Arrange halved cherry tomatoes, thinly sliced red onion, and sliced Kalamata olives over the pizza.

Bake the Pizza:
- Place the pizza in the preheated oven and bake for 12-15 minutes or until the crust is golden and the toppings are heated through.

Finish and Garnish:
- Remove the pizza from the oven. Sprinkle fresh oregano leaves over the hot pizza.
- Drizzle extra virgin olive oil over the pizza.

Slice and Serve:
- Allow the Greek Gyro Pizza with Tzatziki Sauce to cool for a few minutes before slicing. Serve and enjoy this flavorful and Mediterranean-inspired pizza!

This pizza brings the flavors of a classic Greek gyro to your pizza, with marinated chicken, creamy Tzatziki sauce, and a variety of Mediterranean toppings. It's a delicious fusion of two beloved dishes!

Tomato and Olive Fougasse Pizza

For the Fougasse Dough:

- 1 pound pizza dough (homemade or store-bought)
- 1/4 cup olive oil
- 1 teaspoon dried oregano
- 1 teaspoon dried thyme
- 1/2 teaspoon garlic powder
- Salt and black pepper to taste

For the Toppings:

- 1/2 cup pizza sauce or marinara sauce
- 1 1/2 cups shredded mozzarella cheese
- 1 cup cherry tomatoes, halved
- 1/2 cup Kalamata olives, sliced
- 1/4 cup red onion, thinly sliced
- 2 cloves garlic, minced
- Fresh basil leaves for garnish
- Extra virgin olive oil for drizzling

Instructions:

For the Fougasse Dough:

Preheat the Oven:
- Preheat your oven to the highest temperature it can go (usually around 475-500°F or 245-260°C).

Prepare the Dough:
- If using store-bought dough, follow the package instructions for bringing it to room temperature. If making homemade dough, roll it out on a floured surface to your desired thickness.

Shape the Fougasse:
- Combine olive oil, dried oregano, dried thyme, garlic powder, salt, and black pepper in a small bowl.

- Stretch or roll out the pizza dough into an oval shape. Transfer it to a parchment-lined baking sheet.
- Use a sharp knife to make cuts in the dough, creating a leaf-like pattern. Pull the cuts slightly apart to give the dough a fougasse shape.
- Brush the olive oil and herb mixture over the fougasse dough, ensuring it's evenly coated.

Bake the Fougasse:
- Bake the fougasse in the preheated oven for 8-10 minutes or until it starts to firm up and turn golden.

Prepare the Pizza:
- Remove the partially baked fougasse from the oven. Lower the oven temperature to 425°F (220°C).
- Spread pizza sauce evenly over the fougasse, leaving a border around the edges for the crust.
- Sprinkle shredded mozzarella cheese over the sauce.
- Distribute halved cherry tomatoes, sliced Kalamata olives, sliced red onion, and minced garlic evenly over the pizza.

Bake the Pizza:
- Place the pizza back in the oven and bake for an additional 12-15 minutes or until the crust is golden, and the toppings are heated through.

Finish and Garnish:
- Remove the Tomato and Olive Fougasse Pizza from the oven. Sprinkle fresh basil leaves over the hot pizza.
- Drizzle extra virgin olive oil over the pizza.

Slice and Serve:
- Allow the pizza to cool for a few minutes before slicing. Serve and enjoy your flavorful and uniquely shaped Fougasse Pizza!

This pizza combines the artisanal feel of fougasse bread with the classic flavors of tomatoes and olives. It's a perfect choice for those who enjoy a Mediterranean twist on their pizza.

Spanakopita-Inspired Pizza

For the Pizza Dough:

- 1 pound pizza dough (homemade or store-bought)

For the Spanakopita Filling:

- 2 tablespoons olive oil
- 1 small onion, finely chopped
- 2 cloves garlic, minced
- 1 pound fresh spinach, chopped
- 1 cup feta cheese, crumbled
- 1/2 cup ricotta cheese
- 1/4 cup grated Parmesan cheese
- 1 tablespoon fresh dill, chopped
- Salt and black pepper to taste
- Pinch of nutmeg (optional)

For the Pizza:

- 1 cup shredded mozzarella cheese
- 1/4 cup pine nuts, toasted
- Zest of 1 lemon
- Extra virgin olive oil for drizzling
- Red pepper flakes for garnish (optional)

Instructions:

For the Spanakopita Filling:

> Preheat the Oven:
> - Preheat your oven to the highest temperature it can go (usually around 475-500°F or 245-260°C).
>
> Prepare the Filling:
> - In a large skillet, heat olive oil over medium heat. Add chopped onion and sauté until softened.

- Add minced garlic and chopped fresh spinach to the skillet. Cook until the spinach is wilted.
- Remove the skillet from heat and transfer the spinach mixture to a bowl. Allow it to cool slightly.
- To the spinach mixture, add crumbled feta cheese, ricotta cheese, grated Parmesan cheese, chopped fresh dill, salt, black pepper, and nutmeg (if using). Mix well.

For the Pizza:

Preheat the Oven:
- If you haven't already, preheat your oven to the highest temperature it can go.

Prepare the Dough:
- If using store-bought dough, follow the package instructions for bringing it to room temperature. If making homemade dough, roll it out on a floured surface to your desired thickness.

Assemble the Pizza:
- Place the rolled-out pizza dough on a pizza stone or a baking sheet.
- Spread the prepared spanakopita filling evenly over the dough, leaving a border around the edges for the crust.
- Sprinkle shredded mozzarella cheese over the spanakopita filling.
- Toast the pine nuts in a dry pan over medium heat until golden. Sprinkle the toasted pine nuts over the pizza.
- Zest a lemon over the pizza for a burst of freshness.

Bake the Pizza:
- Place the pizza in the preheated oven and bake for 12-15 minutes or until the crust is golden, and the toppings are heated through.

Finish and Garnish:
- Remove the Spanakopita-Inspired Pizza from the oven. Drizzle extra virgin olive oil over the hot pizza.
- Optionally, sprinkle red pepper flakes for a bit of heat.

Slice and Serve:
- Allow the pizza to cool for a few minutes before slicing. Serve and enjoy your unique and flavorful Spanakopita-Inspired Pizza!

This pizza takes inspiration from the classic Greek spanakopita, featuring a spinach and cheese filling on a crispy crust. It's a delightful twist on traditional pizza!

Greek Flatbread Pizza with Sun-Dried Tomatoes

For the Flatbread Dough:

- 1 pound pizza dough (homemade or store-bought)
- 1 tablespoon olive oil
- 1 teaspoon dried oregano
- 1/2 teaspoon garlic powder
- Salt and black pepper to taste

For the Toppings:

- 1/2 cup hummus (store-bought or homemade)
- 1 cup cherry tomatoes, halved
- 1/4 cup sun-dried tomatoes, chopped
- 1/2 cucumber, thinly sliced
- 1/4 red onion, thinly sliced
- 1/2 cup Kalamata olives, sliced
- 1/2 cup crumbled feta cheese
- Fresh parsley or basil for garnish
- Extra virgin olive oil for drizzling

Instructions:

For the Flatbread Dough:

    Preheat the Oven:
- Preheat your oven to the highest temperature it can go (usually around 475-500°F or 245-260°C).

    Prepare the Dough:
- If using store-bought dough, follow the package instructions for bringing it to room temperature. If making homemade dough, roll it out on a floured surface to your desired thickness.

    Assemble the Flatbread:
- Place the rolled-out flatbread dough on a pizza stone or a baking sheet.
- Brush the dough with olive oil and sprinkle dried oregano, garlic powder, salt, and black pepper evenly over the surface.

    Bake the Flatbread:

- Bake the flatbread in the preheated oven for 8-10 minutes or until it starts to firm up and turn golden.

For the Toppings:

Prepare the Toppings:
- Once the flatbread is partially baked, remove it from the oven.
- Spread hummus evenly over the flatbread, leaving a border around the edges for the crust.
- Distribute halved cherry tomatoes, chopped sun-dried tomatoes, thinly sliced cucumber, sliced red onion, and sliced Kalamata olives over the hummus.
- Sprinkle crumbled feta cheese over the toppings.

Finish and Garnish:
- Place the topped flatbread back in the oven and bake for an additional 5-7 minutes or until the crust is golden, and the toppings are heated through.
- Remove the Greek Flatbread Pizza from the oven. Garnish with fresh parsley or basil.
- Drizzle extra virgin olive oil over the hot pizza.

Slice and Serve:
- Allow the pizza to cool for a few minutes before slicing. Serve and enjoy your flavorful Greek Flatbread Pizza with Sun-Dried Tomatoes!

This pizza offers a Greek-inspired twist with the addition of hummus, sun-dried tomatoes, and other Mediterranean toppings. It's a quick and delicious option for a light meal or appetizer.

Lemon and Oregano Chicken Pita Pizza

For the Lemon and Oregano Chicken:

- 1 pound boneless, skinless chicken breasts, thinly sliced
- Zest and juice of 1 lemon
- 2 tablespoons olive oil
- 2 teaspoons dried oregano
- 2 cloves garlic, minced
- Salt and black pepper to taste

For the Pita Pizza:

- 4 whole wheat pita bread rounds
- 1/2 cup Greek yogurt
- 1 tablespoon olive oil
- 1 cup cherry tomatoes, halved
- 1/2 cucumber, thinly sliced
- 1/4 red onion, thinly sliced
- 1/4 cup Kalamata olives, sliced
- Crumbled feta cheese for sprinkling
- Fresh parsley for garnish
- Extra lemon wedges for serving

Instructions:

For the Lemon and Oregano Chicken:

Marinate the Chicken:
- In a bowl, combine the thinly sliced chicken with lemon zest, lemon juice, olive oil, dried oregano, minced garlic, salt, and black pepper. Allow it to marinate for at least 30 minutes.

Cook the Chicken:
- Heat a skillet over medium-high heat. Cook the marinated chicken slices until fully cooked and slightly caramelized. Set aside.

For the Pita Pizza:

Preheat the Oven:
- Preheat your oven to 375°F (190°C).

Prepare the Pita Bread:
- Place the whole wheat pita rounds on a baking sheet.

Make Yogurt Sauce:
- In a small bowl, mix Greek yogurt with olive oil. This will be your sauce for the pita pizza.

Assemble the Pita Pizzas:
- Spread the Greek yogurt and olive oil mixture evenly over each pita round, leaving a border around the edges for the crust.
- Distribute the cooked lemon and oregano chicken over the yogurt-covered pitas.
- Arrange halved cherry tomatoes, thinly sliced cucumber, sliced red onion, and sliced Kalamata olives over the chicken.
- Sprinkle crumbled feta cheese over the toppings.

Bake the Pita Pizzas:
- Place the baking sheet in the preheated oven and bake for 10-12 minutes or until the edges of the pita are golden, and the toppings are heated through.

Finish and Garnish:
- Remove the Lemon and Oregano Chicken Pita Pizzas from the oven. Sprinkle fresh parsley over the hot pizzas.

Serve:
- Serve the pizzas hot, garnished with extra lemon wedges on the side.

Enjoy your Lemon and Oregano Chicken Pita Pizza, a flavorful and Mediterranean-inspired dish!

Mediterranean Seafood Pizza

Ingredients:

For the Pizza Dough:

- 1 pound pizza dough (homemade or store-bought)

For the Tomato Sauce:

- 1 cup tomato sauce
- 2 cloves garlic, minced
- 1 teaspoon dried oregano
- Salt and black pepper to taste

For the Toppings:

- 1/2 cup shredded mozzarella cheese
- 1/2 cup feta cheese, crumbled
- 1/2 cup cooked shrimp, peeled and deveined
- 1/2 cup calamari rings
- 1/4 cup Kalamata olives, sliced
- 1/4 cup sun-dried tomatoes, sliced
- 1/4 cup artichoke hearts, quartered
- 1/4 cup red onion, thinly sliced
- Fresh basil leaves for garnish
- Lemon wedges for serving

Instructions:

Preheat the Oven:
- Preheat your oven to the highest temperature it can go (usually around 475-500°F or 245-260°C).

Prepare the Dough:
- If using store-bought dough, follow the package instructions for bringing it to room temperature. If making homemade dough, roll it out on a floured surface to your desired thickness.

Make Tomato Sauce:
- In a small bowl, mix together tomato sauce, minced garlic, dried oregano, salt, and black pepper to create the pizza sauce.

Assemble the Pizza:
- Place the rolled-out pizza dough on a pizza stone or a baking sheet.
- Spread the tomato sauce evenly over the dough, leaving a border around the edges for the crust.
- Sprinkle shredded mozzarella cheese over the sauce.
- Distribute cooked shrimp, calamari rings, crumbled feta cheese, Kalamata olives, sun-dried tomatoes, artichoke hearts, and thinly sliced red onion over the pizza.

Bake the Pizza:
- Place the pizza in the preheated oven and bake for 12-15 minutes or until the crust is golden, and the seafood is cooked through.

Finish and Garnish:
- Remove the Mediterranean Seafood Pizza from the oven. Sprinkle fresh basil leaves over the hot pizza.
- Serve with lemon wedges on the side for a burst of citrus flavor.

Slice and Serve:
- Allow the pizza to cool for a few minutes before slicing. Serve and enjoy your delicious and Mediterranean-inspired Seafood Pizza!

This pizza brings together the flavors of the Mediterranean with a variety of seafood, feta cheese, and other delightful toppings. It's a perfect choice for seafood and pizza lovers alike!

Roasted Red Pepper and Feta Pizza

Ingredients:

For the Pizza Dough:

- 1 pound pizza dough (homemade or store-bought)
- Cornmeal or flour for dusting

For the Roasted Red Pepper Sauce:

- 2 large red bell peppers
- 2 tablespoons olive oil
- 2 cloves garlic, minced
- Salt and black pepper to taste

For the Pizza:

- 1 cup crumbled feta cheese
- 1 cup shredded mozzarella cheese
- 1/2 cup Kalamata olives, sliced
- 1/4 cup red onion, thinly sliced
- 1/4 cup fresh basil leaves, torn
- Crushed red pepper flakes (optional, for added heat)
- Balsamic glaze for drizzling (optional)

Instructions:

For the Roasted Red Pepper Sauce:

Roast the Red Peppers:
- Preheat your oven broiler. Cut the red bell peppers in half and remove the seeds and membranes.
- Place the pepper halves, skin side up, on a baking sheet. Broil until the skins are blackened and blistered, about 8-10 minutes.
- Remove from the oven, place the peppers in a bowl, and cover with plastic wrap. Let them cool for 10 minutes.
- Peel off the skin from the peppers and discard. Place the roasted peppers in a blender or food processor.

Make the Roasted Red Pepper Sauce:

- Add olive oil, minced garlic, salt, and black pepper to the roasted red peppers in the blender or food processor. Blend until you have a smooth sauce.
- Set the roasted red pepper sauce aside.

For the Pizza:

Preheat the Oven:
- Preheat your oven to the highest temperature it can go (usually around 475-500°F or 245-260°C).

Prepare the Dough:
- If using store-bought dough, follow the package instructions for bringing it to room temperature. If making homemade dough, roll it out on a floured surface to your desired thickness.

Assemble the Pizza:
- Sprinkle cornmeal or flour on a pizza stone or a baking sheet. Place the rolled-out pizza dough on the prepared surface.
- Spread the roasted red pepper sauce evenly over the pizza dough, leaving a border around the edges for the crust.
- Sprinkle crumbled feta cheese and shredded mozzarella cheese over the sauce.
- Distribute sliced Kalamata olives and thinly sliced red onion over the cheese.

Bake the Pizza:
- Place the pizza in the preheated oven and bake for 12-15 minutes or until the crust is golden, and the cheese is melted and bubbly.

Finish and Garnish:
- Remove the Roasted Red Pepper and Feta Pizza from the oven. Sprinkle torn fresh basil leaves over the hot pizza.
- Optionally, drizzle balsamic glaze over the top for added flavor.

Slice and Serve:
- Allow the pizza to cool for a few minutes before slicing. Serve and enjoy this flavorful Roasted Red Pepper and Feta Pizza!

This pizza offers a perfect combination of sweet, tangy roasted red pepper sauce, creamy feta, and a variety of Mediterranean toppings. It's a delightful and easy-to-make option for pizza night!

Grilled Zucchini and Halloumi Pizza

Ingredients:

For the Pizza Dough:

- 1 pound pizza dough (homemade or store-bought)
- Cornmeal or flour for dusting

For the Toppings:

- 1 medium-sized zucchini, thinly sliced
- 8 ounces halloumi cheese, sliced
- 2 tablespoons olive oil
- 2 cloves garlic, minced
- Salt and black pepper to taste

For the Sauce:

- 1/2 cup tomato sauce or marinara sauce

For the Pizza:

- 1 cup shredded mozzarella cheese
- 1/4 cup fresh basil leaves, torn
- Red pepper flakes (optional, for added heat)
- Balsamic glaze for drizzling (optional)

Instructions:

For the Toppings:

    Preheat the Grill:
- Preheat your grill to medium-high heat.

Grill the Zucchini and Halloumi:

- In a bowl, toss the thinly sliced zucchini with olive oil, minced garlic, salt, and black pepper.
- Grill the zucchini slices for 2-3 minutes per side or until they have grill marks and are slightly softened. Remove and set aside.
- Grill the halloumi slices for 1-2 minutes per side or until they are golden brown. Remove and set aside.

For the Pizza:

Preheat the Oven:
- Preheat your oven to the highest temperature it can go (usually around 475-500°F or 245-260°C).

Prepare the Dough:
- Sprinkle cornmeal or flour on a pizza stone or a baking sheet. Place the rolled-out pizza dough on the prepared surface.

Assemble the Pizza:
- Spread tomato sauce evenly over the pizza dough, leaving a border around the edges for the crust.
- Sprinkle shredded mozzarella cheese over the sauce.
- Arrange the grilled zucchini slices and halloumi slices evenly over the cheese.

Bake the Pizza:
- Place the pizza in the preheated oven and bake for 12-15 minutes or until the crust is golden, and the cheese is melted and bubbly.

Finish and Garnish:
- Remove the Grilled Zucchini and Halloumi Pizza from the oven. Sprinkle torn fresh basil leaves over the hot pizza.
- Optionally, sprinkle red pepper flakes for added heat and drizzle balsamic glaze over the top for extra flavor.

Slice and Serve:
- Allow the pizza to cool for a few minutes before slicing. Serve and enjoy your flavorful Grilled Zucchini and Halloumi Pizza!

This pizza combines the smoky flavors of grilled zucchini and halloumi with the classic goodness of melted mozzarella and fresh basil. It's a delightful and unique pizza option!

Greek Eggplant and Tomato Pizza

Ingredients:

For the Pizza Dough:

- 1 pound pizza dough (homemade or store-bought)
- Cornmeal or flour for dusting

For the Toppings:

- 1 medium eggplant, thinly sliced
- 2 tablespoons olive oil
- 2 cloves garlic, minced
- Salt and black pepper to taste
- 1 cup cherry tomatoes, halved
- 1/2 cup crumbled feta cheese
- 1/4 cup Kalamata olives, sliced
- 1/4 cup red onion, thinly sliced
- Fresh oregano leaves for garnish

For the Sauce:

- 1/2 cup tomato sauce or marinara sauce

For the Pizza:

- 1 cup shredded mozzarella cheese
- Extra virgin olive oil for drizzling

Instructions:

For the Toppings:

  Preheat the Oven:
  - Preheat your oven to 425°F (220°C).

Prepare the Eggplant:
- Place the thinly sliced eggplant in a colander and sprinkle with salt. Allow it to sit for about 15 minutes to draw out excess moisture.
- Rinse the eggplant slices under cold water and pat them dry with a paper towel.
- In a bowl, toss the eggplant slices with olive oil, minced garlic, salt, and black pepper.
- Arrange the seasoned eggplant slices on a baking sheet in a single layer. Bake for 15-20 minutes or until the eggplant is tender and golden brown. Set aside.

For the Pizza:

Preheat the Oven:
- Preheat your oven to the highest temperature it can go (usually around 475-500°F or 245-260°C).

Prepare the Dough:
- Sprinkle cornmeal or flour on a pizza stone or a baking sheet. Place the rolled-out pizza dough on the prepared surface.

Assemble the Pizza:
- Spread tomato sauce evenly over the pizza dough, leaving a border around the edges for the crust.
- Sprinkle shredded mozzarella cheese over the sauce.
- Arrange the baked eggplant slices, halved cherry tomatoes, crumbled feta cheese, sliced Kalamata olives, and thinly sliced red onion evenly over the cheese.

Bake the Pizza:
- Place the pizza in the preheated oven and bake for 12-15 minutes or until the crust is golden, and the cheese is melted and bubbly.

Finish and Garnish:
- Remove the Greek Eggplant and Tomato Pizza from the oven. Sprinkle fresh oregano leaves over the hot pizza.
- Drizzle extra virgin olive oil over the pizza.

Slice and Serve:
- Allow the pizza to cool for a few minutes before slicing. Serve and enjoy your flavorful Greek Eggplant and Tomato Pizza!

This pizza captures the essence of Greek cuisine with the combination of roasted eggplant, juicy cherry tomatoes, feta cheese, and olives. It's a delightful and Mediterranean-inspired pizza!

Hummus and Roasted Vegetable Pita Pizza

Ingredients:

For the Roasted Vegetables:

- 1 medium zucchini, sliced
- 1 red bell pepper, sliced
- 1 yellow bell pepper, sliced
- 1 red onion, thinly sliced
- 2 tablespoons olive oil
- 1 teaspoon dried oregano
- Salt and black pepper to taste

For the Pita Pizza:

- 4 whole wheat pita bread rounds
- 1 cup hummus (store-bought or homemade)
- 1 cup cherry tomatoes, halved
- 1/2 cup crumbled feta cheese
- Fresh parsley or basil for garnish
- Extra virgin olive oil for drizzling
- Red pepper flakes (optional, for added heat)

Instructions:

For the Roasted Vegetables:

Preheat the Oven:
- Preheat your oven to 425°F (220°C).

Prepare the Vegetables:
- In a large bowl, toss the sliced zucchini, red bell pepper, yellow bell pepper, and red onion with olive oil, dried oregano, salt, and black pepper.
- Spread the seasoned vegetables on a baking sheet in a single layer.

Roast the Vegetables:
- Roast the vegetables in the preheated oven for 20-25 minutes or until they are tender and slightly caramelized. Stir the vegetables halfway through the roasting time.
- Remove the roasted vegetables from the oven and set aside.

For the Pita Pizza:

- Preheat the Oven:
  - Preheat your oven to 375°F (190°C).
- Assemble the Pita Pizzas:
  - Place the whole wheat pita rounds on a baking sheet.
  - Spread a generous layer of hummus over each pita round, leaving a border around the edges for the crust.
  - Arrange the roasted vegetables evenly over the hummus-covered pitas.
  - Sprinkle halved cherry tomatoes and crumbled feta cheese over the vegetables.
- Bake the Pita Pizzas:
  - Place the baking sheet in the preheated oven and bake for 10-12 minutes or until the edges of the pita are golden, and the toppings are heated through.
- Finish and Garnish:
  - Remove the Hummus and Roasted Vegetable Pita Pizzas from the oven. Sprinkle fresh parsley or basil over the hot pizzas.
  - Drizzle extra virgin olive oil over the pizzas.
  - Optionally, sprinkle red pepper flakes for added heat.
- Slice and Serve:
  - Allow the pizzas to cool for a few minutes before slicing. Serve and enjoy your flavorful Hummus and Roasted Vegetable Pita Pizzas!

This pizza combines the creaminess of hummus with the savory goodness of roasted vegetables for a satisfying and healthy meal. It's perfect for a quick and tasty lunch or dinner!

Greek Shrimp Scampi Pizza

Ingredients:

For the Pizza Dough:

- 1 pound pizza dough (homemade or store-bought)
- Cornmeal or flour for dusting

For the Shrimp Scampi:

- 1 pound large shrimp, peeled and deveined
- 4 tablespoons unsalted butter
- 4 tablespoons olive oil
- 4 cloves garlic, minced
- 1/2 teaspoon red pepper flakes (adjust to taste)
- Zest and juice of 1 lemon
- Salt and black pepper to taste
- 1/4 cup fresh parsley, chopped

For the Pizza:

- 1 cup shredded mozzarella cheese
- 1/2 cup crumbled feta cheese
- 1/4 cup Kalamata olives, sliced
- 1/4 cup red onion, thinly sliced
- 1/4 cup cherry tomatoes, halved
- 1/4 cup fresh parsley, chopped
- Extra virgin olive oil for drizzling

Instructions:

For the Shrimp Scampi:

    Prepare the Shrimp:
- Pat the shrimp dry and season with salt and black pepper.

    Cook the Shrimp:
- In a large skillet over medium heat, melt butter and olive oil.
- Add minced garlic and red pepper flakes to the skillet. Sauté for about 1 minute until fragrant.

- Add the shrimp to the skillet and cook for 2-3 minutes per side or until they turn pink and opaque.
- Stir in lemon zest, lemon juice, and chopped fresh parsley. Remove from heat and set aside.

For the Pizza:

Preheat the Oven:
- Preheat your oven to the highest temperature it can go (usually around 475-500°F or 245-260°C).

Prepare the Dough:
- Sprinkle cornmeal or flour on a pizza stone or a baking sheet. Place the rolled-out pizza dough on the prepared surface.

Assemble the Pizza:
- Spread shredded mozzarella cheese evenly over the pizza dough, leaving a border around the edges for the crust.
- Arrange the cooked shrimp scampi over the cheese.
- Sprinkle crumbled feta cheese, sliced Kalamata olives, thinly sliced red onion, and halved cherry tomatoes over the pizza.

Bake the Pizza:
- Place the pizza in the preheated oven and bake for 12-15 minutes or until the crust is golden, and the cheese is melted and bubbly.

Finish and Garnish:
- Remove the Greek Shrimp Scampi Pizza from the oven. Sprinkle fresh chopped parsley over the hot pizza.
- Drizzle extra virgin olive oil over the pizza.

Slice and Serve:
- Allow the pizza to cool for a few minutes before slicing. Serve and enjoy your flavorful Greek Shrimp Scampi Pizza!

This pizza brings the flavors of shrimp scampi together with Mediterranean toppings, creating a delightful and savory dish that's perfect for seafood lovers!

Greek-Style Lamb Meatball Pizza

Ingredients:

For the Lamb Meatballs:

- 1 pound ground lamb
- 1/2 cup breadcrumbs
- 1/4 cup crumbled feta cheese
- 1/4 cup finely chopped red onion
- 2 cloves garlic, minced
- 1 teaspoon dried oregano
- 1 teaspoon ground cumin
- Salt and black pepper to taste
- 1 large egg
- Olive oil for cooking

For the Pizza Dough:

- 1 pound pizza dough (homemade or store-bought)
- Cornmeal or flour for dusting

For the Tzatziki Sauce:

- 1 cup Greek yogurt
- 1/2 cucumber, grated and drained
- 2 cloves garlic, minced
- 1 tablespoon fresh dill, chopped
- 1 tablespoon extra virgin olive oil
- Salt and black pepper to taste

For the Pizza:

- 1 cup cherry tomatoes, halved
- 1/2 cup Kalamata olives, sliced
- 1/4 cup red onion, thinly sliced
- 1 cup shredded mozzarella cheese

- Crumbled feta cheese for sprinkling
- Fresh mint leaves for garnish
- Extra virgin olive oil for drizzling

Instructions:

For the Lamb Meatballs:

Preheat the Oven:
- Preheat your oven to 400°F (200°C).

Prepare the Meatball Mixture:
- In a large bowl, combine ground lamb, breadcrumbs, crumbled feta cheese, chopped red onion, minced garlic, dried oregano, ground cumin, salt, black pepper, and the egg.
- Mix until well combined.

Form the Meatballs:
- Shape the mixture into small meatballs, about 1 inch in diameter.

Cook the Meatballs:
- Heat olive oil in an oven-safe skillet over medium-high heat.
- Brown the meatballs on all sides in the skillet.
- Transfer the skillet to the preheated oven and bake for 12-15 minutes or until the meatballs are cooked through.

For the Tzatziki Sauce:

Prepare the Tzatziki:
- In a bowl, combine Greek yogurt, grated and drained cucumber, minced garlic, chopped fresh dill, extra virgin olive oil, salt, and black pepper. Mix well.
- Refrigerate the tzatziki sauce until ready to use.

For the Pizza:

Preheat the Oven:
- Preheat your oven to the highest temperature it can go (usually around 475-500°F or 245-260°C).

Prepare the Dough:

- Sprinkle cornmeal or flour on a pizza stone or a baking sheet. Place the rolled-out pizza dough on the prepared surface.

Assemble the Pizza:
- Spread a layer of tzatziki sauce evenly over the pizza dough, leaving a border around the edges for the crust.
- Arrange the cooked lamb meatballs over the tzatziki-covered dough.
- Scatter halved cherry tomatoes, sliced Kalamata olives, and thinly sliced red onion over the pizza.
- Sprinkle shredded mozzarella cheese over the toppings.

Bake the Pizza:
- Place the pizza in the preheated oven and bake for 12-15 minutes or until the crust is golden, and the cheese is melted and bubbly.

Finish and Garnish:
- Remove the Greek-Style Lamb Meatball Pizza from the oven. Sprinkle crumbled feta cheese over the hot pizza.
- Garnish with fresh mint leaves and drizzle extra virgin olive oil over the pizza.

Slice and Serve:
- Allow the pizza to cool for a few minutes before slicing. Serve and enjoy your flavorful Greek-Style Lamb Meatball Pizza!

This pizza combines the rich flavors of lamb meatballs with traditional Greek ingredients for a delicious and Mediterranean-inspired dish.

Chickpea and Feta Pita Pizza

Ingredients:

For the Chickpea Topping:

- 1 can (15 ounces) chickpeas, drained and rinsed
- 2 tablespoons olive oil
- 1 teaspoon smoked paprika
- 1/2 teaspoon ground cumin
- 1/2 teaspoon garlic powder
- Salt and black pepper to taste

For the Pita Pizza:

- 4 whole wheat pita bread rounds
- 1/2 cup tomato sauce or marinara sauce
- 1 cup crumbled feta cheese
- 1/2 cup cherry tomatoes, halved
- 1/4 cup Kalamata olives, sliced
- 1/4 cup red onion, thinly sliced
- Fresh parsley or basil for garnish
- Extra virgin olive oil for drizzling
- Red pepper flakes (optional, for added heat)

Instructions:

For the Chickpea Topping:

Preheat the Oven:
- Preheat your oven to 400°F (200°C).

Prepare the Chickpeas:
- In a bowl, toss the chickpeas with olive oil, smoked paprika, ground cumin, garlic powder, salt, and black pepper until well coated.

Roast the Chickpeas:
- Spread the seasoned chickpeas on a baking sheet in a single layer.
- Roast in the preheated oven for 20-25 minutes or until the chickpeas are crispy and golden brown. Stir them halfway through the roasting time.
- Remove from the oven and set aside.

For the Pita Pizza:

Preheat the Oven:
- Preheat your oven to 375°F (190°C).

Assemble the Pita Pizzas:
- Place the whole wheat pita rounds on a baking sheet.
- Spread a layer of tomato sauce or marinara sauce over each pita round, leaving a border around the edges for the crust.
- Sprinkle crumbled feta cheese over the sauce.
- Distribute the roasted chickpeas, halved cherry tomatoes, sliced Kalamata olives, and thinly sliced red onion evenly over the pizzas.

Bake the Pita Pizzas:
- Place the baking sheet in the preheated oven and bake for 10-12 minutes or until the edges of the pita are golden, and the toppings are heated through.

Finish and Garnish:
- Remove the Chickpea and Feta Pita Pizzas from the oven. Sprinkle fresh parsley or basil over the hot pizzas.
- Drizzle extra virgin olive oil over the pizzas.
- Optionally, sprinkle red pepper flakes for added heat.

Slice and Serve:
- Allow the pizzas to cool for a few minutes before slicing. Serve and enjoy your flavorful Chickpea and Feta Pita Pizzas!

This pizza offers a delightful combination of crispy roasted chickpeas, tangy feta cheese, and Mediterranean toppings on a whole wheat pita. It's a quick and nutritious option for a light meal or snack!

Mediterranean Pesto Pizza

Ingredients:

For the Pesto Sauce:

- 2 cups fresh basil leaves, packed
- 1/2 cup pine nuts, toasted
- 1/2 cup grated Parmesan cheese
- 3 cloves garlic, minced
- 1/2 cup extra virgin olive oil
- Salt and black pepper to taste

For the Pizza:

- 1 pound pizza dough (homemade or store-bought)
- Cornmeal or flour for dusting
- 1 cup cherry tomatoes, halved
- 1/2 cup Kalamata olives, sliced
- 1/4 cup red onion, thinly sliced
- 1/2 cup crumbled feta cheese
- 1/2 cup shredded mozzarella cheese
- 1/4 cup sun-dried tomatoes, thinly sliced
- Fresh oregano or basil for garnish
- Extra virgin olive oil for drizzling

Instructions:

For the Pesto Sauce:

Prepare the Pesto:
- In a food processor, combine fresh basil leaves, toasted pine nuts, grated Parmesan cheese, minced garlic, salt, and black pepper.
- Pulse the ingredients until coarsely chopped.
- With the food processor running, slowly pour in the extra virgin olive oil until the pesto reaches a smooth and creamy consistency.
- Adjust salt and pepper to taste. Set the pesto aside.

For the Pizza:

Preheat the Oven:
- Preheat your oven to the highest temperature it can go (usually around 475-500°F or 245-260°C).

Prepare the Dough:
- Sprinkle cornmeal or flour on a pizza stone or a baking sheet. Place the rolled-out pizza dough on the prepared surface.

Assemble the Pizza:
- Spread a generous layer of the prepared pesto sauce over the pizza dough, leaving a border around the edges for the crust.
- Sprinkle shredded mozzarella cheese evenly over the pesto.
- Scatter halved cherry tomatoes, sliced Kalamata olives, thinly sliced red onion, crumbled feta cheese, and sun-dried tomatoes over the pizza.

Bake the Pizza:
- Place the pizza in the preheated oven and bake for 12-15 minutes or until the crust is golden, and the cheese is melted and bubbly.

Finish and Garnish:
- Remove the Mediterranean Pesto Pizza from the oven. Sprinkle fresh oregano or basil over the hot pizza.
- Drizzle extra virgin olive oil over the pizza.

Slice and Serve:
- Allow the pizza to cool for a few minutes before slicing. Serve and enjoy your flavorful Mediterranean Pesto Pizza!

This pizza is bursting with the vibrant flavors of homemade pesto and Mediterranean toppings. It's a delightful and fresh twist on traditional pizza!

Greek Chicken and Olive Naan Pizza

Ingredients:

For the Greek Chicken:

- 1 pound boneless, skinless chicken breasts, thinly sliced
- 2 tablespoons olive oil
- 1 teaspoon dried oregano
- 1 teaspoon dried thyme
- 1 teaspoon garlic powder
- Salt and black pepper to taste
- Juice of 1 lemon

For the Pizza:

- 4 pieces of naan bread
- 1 cup Tzatziki sauce (store-bought or homemade)
- 1 cup cherry tomatoes, halved
- 1/2 cup Kalamata olives, sliced
- 1/4 cup red onion, thinly sliced
- 1 cup crumbled feta cheese
- Fresh parsley for garnish
- Extra virgin olive oil for drizzling

Instructions:

For the Greek Chicken:

Marinate the Chicken:
- In a bowl, combine sliced chicken breasts with olive oil, dried oregano, dried thyme, garlic powder, salt, black pepper, and lemon juice. Toss until the chicken is well coated.

Cook the Chicken:
- Heat a skillet over medium-high heat. Add the marinated chicken slices and cook for 5-7 minutes or until the chicken is fully cooked and slightly browned. Set aside.

For the Pizza:

- Preheat the Oven:
    - Preheat your oven to 400°F (200°C).
- Assemble the Naan Pizzas:
    - Place the naan bread on a baking sheet.
    - Spread a layer of Tzatziki sauce over each naan bread, leaving a border around the edges for the crust.
    - Distribute the cooked Greek chicken evenly over the Tzatziki-covered naan bread.
    - Scatter halved cherry tomatoes, sliced Kalamata olives, and thinly sliced red onion over the pizzas.
    - Sprinkle crumbled feta cheese over the toppings.
- Bake the Naan Pizzas:
    - Place the baking sheet in the preheated oven and bake for 10-12 minutes or until the edges of the naan are golden, and the toppings are heated through.
- Finish and Garnish:
    - Remove the Greek Chicken and Olive Naan Pizzas from the oven. Sprinkle fresh parsley over the hot pizzas.
    - Drizzle extra virgin olive oil over the pizzas.
- Slice and Serve:
    - Allow the pizzas to cool for a few minutes before slicing. Serve and enjoy your flavorful Greek Chicken and Olive Naan Pizzas!

This pizza combines the Mediterranean flavors of Greek chicken, olives, feta, and Tzatziki on a convenient and delicious naan bread crust. It's a quick and satisfying meal for lunch or dinner!

Spinach and Feta Stuffed Crust Pizza

Ingredients:

For the Stuffed Crust:

- 1 pound pizza dough (homemade or store-bought)
- 8 ounces mozzarella cheese, cut into string cheese sticks
- 1/4 cup grated Parmesan cheese
- 1 teaspoon garlic powder
- 1/2 teaspoon dried oregano
- Olive oil for brushing

For the Pizza:

- 1 cup tomato sauce or marinara sauce
- 2 cups fresh spinach, chopped
- 1 cup feta cheese, crumbled
- 1/2 cup black olives, sliced
- 1/4 cup red onion, thinly sliced
- Crushed red pepper flakes (optional, for added heat)
- Fresh basil leaves for garnish
- Olive oil for drizzling

Instructions:

For the Stuffed Crust:

Preheat the Oven:
- Preheat your oven to 425°F (220°C).

Prepare the Pizza Dough:
- Roll out the pizza dough on a lightly floured surface to your desired size and thickness.

Prepare the Stuffed Crust:
- Place the mozzarella string cheese sticks around the edges of the rolled-out pizza dough, leaving some space at the edges for sealing.
- Fold the dough over the cheese sticks and press to seal, creating a stuffed crust.

- In a small bowl, mix grated Parmesan cheese, garlic powder, and dried oregano. Brush the stuffed crust with olive oil and sprinkle the Parmesan mixture over the edges.

Bake the Stuffed Crust:
- Place the prepared pizza on a baking sheet or pizza stone.
- Bake in the preheated oven for 8-10 minutes or until the crust begins to set but is not fully cooked.

For the Pizza:

Assemble the Pizza:
- Remove the partially baked pizza from the oven.
- Spread tomato sauce over the center of the pizza, leaving the stuffed crust exposed.
- Sprinkle chopped fresh spinach, crumbled feta cheese, sliced black olives, and thinly sliced red onion over the sauce.
- Optionally, sprinkle crushed red pepper flakes for added heat.

Finish Baking:
- Return the pizza to the oven and bake for an additional 10-15 minutes or until the crust is golden, the cheese is melted, and the toppings are cooked.

Garnish and Serve:
- Remove the Spinach and Feta Stuffed Crust Pizza from the oven. Garnish with fresh basil leaves.
- Drizzle olive oil over the pizza.

Slice and Serve:
- Allow the pizza to cool for a few minutes before slicing. Serve and enjoy your delicious Spinach and Feta Stuffed Crust Pizza!

This pizza features a cheesy stuffed crust filled with mozzarella, and the combination of spinach and feta adds a delightful Mediterranean twist. It's a flavorful and satisfying pizza option!

Mediterranean Fig and Prosciutto Pizza

Ingredients:

For the Pizza Dough:

- 1 pound pizza dough (homemade or store-bought)
- Cornmeal or flour for dusting

For the Pizza:

- 1/2 cup fig jam
- 8 ounces fresh mozzarella, sliced
- 4-6 slices prosciutto
- 1/2 cup crumbled goat cheese
- 1/4 cup chopped walnuts
- Fresh arugula for topping
- Balsamic glaze for drizzling
- Olive oil for brushing
- Salt and black pepper to taste

Instructions:

Preheat the Oven:
- Preheat your oven to the highest temperature it can go (usually around 475-500°F or 245-260°C).

Prepare the Dough:
- Sprinkle cornmeal or flour on a pizza stone or a baking sheet. Place the rolled-out pizza dough on the prepared surface.

Assemble the Pizza:
- Spread fig jam evenly over the pizza dough, leaving a border around the edges for the crust.
- Arrange slices of fresh mozzarella over the fig jam.
- Tear prosciutto into smaller pieces and scatter them over the mozzarella.
- Sprinkle crumbled goat cheese and chopped walnuts over the pizza.

Bake the Pizza:
- Place the pizza in the preheated oven and bake for 12-15 minutes or until the crust is golden, and the cheese is melted and bubbly.

Finish and Garnish:

- Remove the Mediterranean Fig and Prosciutto Pizza from the oven.
- Top the hot pizza with fresh arugula.
- Drizzle olive oil and balsamic glaze over the pizza.

Season and Serve:
- Season the pizza with salt and black pepper to taste.
- Allow the pizza to cool for a few minutes before slicing. Serve and enjoy your flavorful Mediterranean Fig and Prosciutto Pizza!

This pizza combines the sweetness of fig jam with the saltiness of prosciutto and the creaminess of goat cheese, creating a delicious Mediterranean-inspired flavor. The addition of fresh arugula and balsamic glaze adds a burst of freshness to each bite!

Greek Bruschetta Pizza

Ingredients:

For the Pizza Dough:

- 1 pound pizza dough (homemade or store-bought)
- Cornmeal or flour for dusting

For the Tzatziki Sauce:

- 1 cup Greek yogurt
- 1/2 cucumber, grated and drained
- 2 cloves garlic, minced
- 1 tablespoon fresh dill, chopped
- 1 tablespoon extra virgin olive oil
- Salt and black pepper to taste

For the Pizza:

- 1 cup cherry tomatoes, diced
- 1/2 cup Kalamata olives, sliced
- 1/4 cup red onion, finely chopped
- 1/2 cup crumbled feta cheese
- 1 tablespoon fresh oregano, chopped
- Extra virgin olive oil for drizzling

Instructions:

For the Tzatziki Sauce:

Prepare the Tzatziki:
- In a bowl, combine Greek yogurt, grated and drained cucumber, minced garlic, chopped fresh dill, extra virgin olive oil, salt, and black pepper. Mix well.
- Refrigerate the tzatziki sauce until ready to use.

For the Pizza:

Preheat the Oven:

- Preheat your oven to the highest temperature it can go (usually around 475-500°F or 245-260°C)

Prepare the Dough:
- Sprinkle cornmeal or flour on a pizza stone or a baking sheet. Place the rolled-out pizza dough on the prepared surface.

Assemble the Pizza:
- Spread a generous layer of tzatziki sauce over the pizza dough, leaving a border around the edges for the crust.
- Scatter diced cherry tomatoes, sliced Kalamata olives, and finely chopped red onion over the tzatziki-covered dough.
- Sprinkle crumbled feta cheese evenly over the toppings.

Bake the Pizza:
- Place the pizza in the preheated oven and bake for 12-15 minutes or until the crust is golden, and the cheese is melted and bubbly.

Finish and Garnish:
- Remove the Greek Bruschetta Pizza from the oven. Sprinkle fresh oregano over the hot pizza.
- Drizzle extra virgin olive oil over the pizza.

Slice and Serve:
- Allow the pizza to cool for a few minutes before slicing. Serve and enjoy your flavorful Greek Bruschetta Pizza!

This pizza combines the traditional flavors of Greek bruschetta with the creamy goodness of tzatziki sauce, making it a refreshing and Mediterranean-inspired dish!

Mediterranean Turkey and Spinach Pizza

Ingredients:

For the Pizza Dough:

- 1 pound pizza dough (homemade or store-bought)
- Cornmeal or flour for dusting

For the Tzatziki Sauce:

- 1 cup Greek yogurt
- 1/2 cucumber, grated and drained
- 2 cloves garlic, minced
- 1 tablespoon fresh dill, chopped
- 1 tablespoon extra virgin olive oil
- Salt and black pepper to taste

For the Pizza:

- 1/2 pound ground turkey
- 1 tablespoon olive oil
- 1 teaspoon dried oregano
- 1/2 teaspoon garlic powder
- Salt and black pepper to taste
- 2 cups fresh spinach, chopped
- 1 cup cherry tomatoes, halved
- 1/2 cup Kalamata olives, sliced
- 1/4 cup red onion, thinly sliced
- 1 cup feta cheese, crumbled
- Extra virgin olive oil for drizzling

Instructions:

For the Tzatziki Sauce:

    Prepare the Tzatziki:

- In a bowl, combine Greek yogurt, grated and drained cucumber, minced garlic, chopped fresh dill, extra virgin olive oil, salt, and black pepper. Mix well.
- Refrigerate the tzatziki sauce until ready to use.

For the Pizza:

Preheat the Oven:
- Preheat your oven to the highest temperature it can go (usually around 475-500°F or 245-260°C).

Prepare the Dough:
- Sprinkle cornmeal or flour on a pizza stone or a baking sheet. Place the rolled-out pizza dough on the prepared surface.

Cook the Ground Turkey:
- In a skillet over medium heat, heat olive oil. Add ground turkey, dried oregano, garlic powder, salt, and black pepper. Cook until the turkey is browned and cooked through. Set aside.

Assemble the Pizza:
- Spread a generous layer of tzatziki sauce over the pizza dough, leaving a border around the edges for the crust.
- Evenly distribute the cooked ground turkey over the tzatziki-covered dough.
- Scatter chopped fresh spinach, halved cherry tomatoes, sliced Kalamata olives, and thinly sliced red onion over the pizza.
- Sprinkle crumbled feta cheese evenly over the toppings.

Bake the Pizza:
- Place the pizza in the preheated oven and bake for 12-15 minutes or until the crust is golden, and the cheese is melted and bubbly.

Finish and Garnish:
- Remove the Mediterranean Turkey and Spinach Pizza from the oven. Drizzle extra virgin olive oil over the pizza.

Slice and Serve:
- Allow the pizza to cool for a few minutes before slicing. Serve and enjoy your flavorful Mediterranean Turkey and Spinach Pizza!

This pizza offers a delightful combination of ground turkey, fresh vegetables, and the creaminess of tzatziki sauce, creating a delicious and Mediterranean-inspired dish!

Greek Spanakopita Pizza Rolls

Ingredients:

For the Filling:

- 1 tablespoon olive oil
- 1 small onion, finely chopped
- 2 cloves garlic, minced
- 8 cups fresh spinach, chopped
- 1 cup feta cheese, crumbled
- 1 cup ricotta cheese
- 1/4 cup grated Parmesan cheese
- 1 teaspoon dried dill
- Salt and black pepper to taste
- 1 tablespoon lemon juice

For the Pizza Rolls:

- 1 pound pizza dough (homemade or store-bought)
- 1/4 cup melted butter
- 1/4 cup grated Parmesan cheese
- Tzatziki sauce for dipping (optional)

Instructions:

For the Filling:

Prepare the Spinach Filling:
- In a large skillet, heat olive oil over medium heat. Add chopped onion and garlic, sautéing until softened.
- Add chopped spinach to the skillet and cook until wilted. Drain excess liquid.
- In a large bowl, combine the sautéed spinach mixture with crumbled feta cheese, ricotta cheese, grated Parmesan cheese, dried dill, salt, black pepper, and lemon juice. Mix well.

For the Pizza Rolls:

- Preheat the Oven:
  - Preheat your oven to 375°F (190°C).
- Prepare the Dough:
  - Roll out the pizza dough on a lightly floured surface to a rectangular shape.
- Assemble the Pizza Rolls:
  - Spread the spinach and cheese filling evenly over the rolled-out pizza dough.
  - Starting from one end, tightly roll the dough to form a log.
  - Using a sharp knife, slice the log into 1-inch thick rounds to create pizza rolls.
- Bake the Pizza Rolls:
  - Place the pizza rolls on a baking sheet lined with parchment paper.
  - Brush the tops of the rolls with melted butter and sprinkle grated Parmesan cheese over them.
  - Bake in the preheated oven for 20-25 minutes or until the rolls are golden brown and cooked through.
- Serve and Dip:
  - Remove the Greek Spanakopita Pizza Rolls from the oven. Serve warm.
  - Optionally, serve with Tzatziki sauce for dipping.

These Greek Spanakopita Pizza Rolls are a delightful fusion of Greek flavors and the convenience of pizza rolls. They make for a tasty appetizer or snack!

Quinoa and Olive Greek Pizza

Ingredients:

For the Pizza Dough:

- 1 pound pizza dough (homemade or store-bought)
- Cornmeal or flour for dusting

For the Tzatziki Sauce:

- 1 cup Greek yogurt
- 1/2 cucumber, grated and drained
- 2 cloves garlic, minced
- 1 tablespoon fresh dill, chopped
- 1 tablespoon extra virgin olive oil
- Salt and black pepper to taste

For the Pizza:

- 1 cup cooked quinoa
- 1/2 cup Kalamata olives, sliced
- 1/4 cup red onion, thinly sliced
- 1 cup cherry tomatoes, halved
- 1/2 cup crumbled feta cheese
- 1/4 cup fresh parsley, chopped
- Extra virgin olive oil for drizzling

Instructions:

For the Tzatziki Sauce:

Prepare the Tzatziki:
- In a bowl, combine Greek yogurt, grated and drained cucumber, minced garlic, chopped fresh dill, extra virgin olive oil, salt, and black pepper. Mix well.
- Refrigerate the tzatziki sauce until ready to use.

For the Pizza:

Preheat the Oven:
- Preheat your oven to the highest temperature it can go (usually around 475-500°F or 245-260°C).

Prepare the Dough:
- Sprinkle cornmeal or flour on a pizza stone or a baking sheet. Place the rolled-out pizza dough on the prepared surface.

Assemble the Pizza:
- Spread a generous layer of tzatziki sauce over the pizza dough, leaving a border around the edges for the crust.
- Evenly distribute the cooked quinoa over the tzatziki-covered dough.
- Scatter sliced Kalamata olives, thinly sliced red onion, and halved cherry tomatoes over the pizza.
- Sprinkle crumbled feta cheese over the toppings.

Bake the Pizza:
- Place the pizza in the preheated oven and bake for 12-15 minutes or until the crust is golden, and the cheese is melted and bubbly.

Finish and Garnish:
- Remove the Quinoa and Olive Greek Pizza from the oven. Sprinkle fresh chopped parsley over the hot pizza.
- Drizzle extra virgin olive oil over the pizza.

Slice and Serve:
- Allow the pizza to cool for a few minutes before slicing. Serve and enjoy your flavorful Quinoa and Olive Greek Pizza!

This pizza combines the nuttiness of quinoa with the Mediterranean flavors of olives, feta, and tzatziki sauce, creating a unique and nutritious twist on the classic Greek pizza!

Greek Moussaka Pizza

Ingredients:

For the Pizza Dough:

- 1 pound pizza dough (homemade or store-bought)
- Cornmeal or flour for dusting

For the Bechamel Sauce:

- 2 tablespoons unsalted butter
- 2 tablespoons all-purpose flour
- 1 cup whole milk
- 1/4 teaspoon ground nutmeg
- Salt and black pepper to taste

For the Pizza Toppings:

- 1/2 pound ground lamb or beef
- 1 onion, finely chopped
- 2 cloves garlic, minced
- 1 eggplant, thinly sliced
- 1 zucchini, thinly sliced
- 1/2 cup tomato sauce
- 1 teaspoon dried oregano
- 1/2 cup crumbled feta cheese
- 1/4 cup grated Parmesan cheese
- Fresh parsley for garnish
- Olive oil for drizzling

Instructions:

For the Bechamel Sauce:

Prepare the Bechamel:
- In a saucepan, melt butter over medium heat. Add flour and whisk continuously to form a smooth paste (roux).
- Gradually add the milk, whisking constantly to avoid lumps.

- Continue cooking and stirring until the sauce thickens. Season with ground nutmeg, salt, and black pepper. Set aside.

For the Pizza Toppings:

Preheat the Oven:
- Preheat your oven to the highest temperature it can go (usually around 475-500°F or 245-260°C).

Prepare the Dough:
- Sprinkle cornmeal or flour on a pizza stone or a baking sheet. Place the rolled-out pizza dough on the prepared surface.

Cook the Ground Meat:
- In a skillet over medium heat, cook the ground lamb or beef until browned. Remove excess fat.

Saute the Vegetables:
- In the same skillet, add chopped onion and minced garlic. Cook until softened.
- Add thinly sliced eggplant and zucchini to the skillet. Cook until the vegetables are tender.

Assemble the Pizza:
- Spread a layer of tomato sauce over the pizza dough, leaving a border around the edges for the crust.
- Distribute the cooked ground meat and sautéed vegetables evenly over the sauce.
- Pour the prepared bechamel sauce over the toppings.
- Sprinkle dried oregano, crumbled feta cheese, and grated Parmesan cheese over the pizza.

Bake the Pizza:
- Place the pizza in the preheated oven and bake for 12-15 minutes or until the crust is golden, and the cheese is melted and bubbly.

Finish and Garnish:
- Remove the Greek Moussaka Pizza from the oven. Sprinkle fresh parsley over the hot pizza.
- Drizzle olive oil over the pizza.

Slice and Serve:
- Allow the pizza to cool for a few minutes before slicing. Serve and enjoy your flavorful Greek Moussaka Pizza!

This pizza captures the essence of Greek moussaka with layers of meat, vegetables, and a creamy bechamel sauce, all on a delicious pizza crust. It's a delightful fusion of flavors!

Grilled Greek Pizza Skewers

Ingredients:

For the Pizza Skewers:

- 1 pound pizza dough (homemade or store-bought)
- Olive oil for brushing
- 1 cup cherry tomatoes
- 1/2 cup Kalamata olives, pitted
- 1/2 cup red onion, cut into chunks
- 1/2 cup feta cheese, cubed
- Fresh oregano for garnish

For the Tzatziki Sauce:

- 1 cup Greek yogurt
- 1/2 cucumber, grated and drained
- 2 cloves garlic, minced

- 1 tablespoon fresh dill, chopped
- 1 tablespoon extra virgin olive oil
- Salt and black pepper to taste

Instructions:

For the Tzatziki Sauce:

Prepare the Tzatziki:
- In a bowl, combine Greek yogurt, grated and drained cucumber, minced garlic, chopped fresh dill, extra virgin olive oil, salt, and black pepper. Mix well.
- Refrigerate the tzatziki sauce until ready to use.

For the Pizza Skewers:

Preheat the Grill:
- Preheat your grill to medium-high heat.

Prepare the Pizza Dough:
- Roll out the pizza dough on a lightly floured surface. Cut the dough into small squares or rectangles, approximately 1-inch in size.
- Brush each piece of pizza dough with olive oil.

Assemble the Skewers:
- Thread the olive oil-brushed pizza dough, cherry tomatoes, Kalamata olives, red onion chunks, and feta cheese cubes onto skewers, alternating the ingredients.

Grill the Skewers:
- Place the assembled skewers on the preheated grill.
- Grill for 3-5 minutes per side or until the pizza dough is cooked and has grill marks.

Finish and Garnish:
- Remove the grilled pizza skewers from the grill.
- Sprinkle fresh oregano over the skewers.

Serve with Tzatziki:
- Serve the grilled Greek pizza skewers with the prepared tzatziki sauce for dipping.

Enjoy:

- Enjoy your delicious Grilled Greek Pizza Skewers as a flavorful appetizer or snack!

These skewers capture the essence of Greek flavors with the combination of grilled pizza dough, cherry tomatoes, olives, red onion, and feta cheese. The tzatziki sauce adds a refreshing touch to complete the dish!

Mediterranean Tuna and Red Onion Pizza

Ingredients:

For the Pizza Dough:

- 1 pound pizza dough (homemade or store-bought)
- Cornmeal or flour for dusting

For the Tomato Sauce:

- 1/2 cup tomato sauce
- 1 tablespoon tomato paste
- 1 clove garlic, minced
- 1 teaspoon dried oregano
- Salt and black pepper to taste

For the Pizza Toppings:

- 1 can (5 ounces) tuna, drained
- 1/2 red onion, thinly sliced
- 1/2 cup Kalamata olives, sliced
- 1/2 cup feta cheese, crumbled
- Fresh parsley, chopped, for garnish
- Lemon wedges for serving

Instructions:

For the Tomato Sauce:

Prepare the Tomato Sauce:
- In a bowl, mix together tomato sauce, tomato paste, minced garlic, dried oregano, salt, and black pepper. Set aside.

For the Pizza:

Preheat the Oven:
- Preheat your oven to the highest temperature it can go (usually around 475-500°F or 245-260°C).

Prepare the Dough:

- Sprinkle cornmeal or flour on a pizza stone or a baking sheet. Place the rolled-out pizza dough on the prepared surface.

Assemble the Pizza:
- Spread a layer of the prepared tomato sauce over the pizza dough, leaving a border around the edges for the crust.
- Evenly distribute the drained tuna over the sauce.
- Scatter thinly sliced red onion and Kalamata olives over the pizza.
- Sprinkle crumbled feta cheese over the toppings.

Bake the Pizza:
- Place the pizza in the preheated oven and bake for 12-15 minutes or until the crust is golden, and the cheese is melted and bubbly.

Finish and Garnish:
- Remove the Mediterranean Tuna and Red Onion Pizza from the oven. Sprinkle fresh chopped parsley over the hot pizza.

Serve with Lemon Wedges:
- Serve the pizza slices with lemon wedges on the side for squeezing over the tuna.

Slice and Enjoy:
- Allow the pizza to cool for a few minutes before slicing. Serve and enjoy your flavorful Mediterranean Tuna and Red Onion Pizza!

This pizza features the richness of tuna combined with the bold flavors of red onion, Kalamata olives, and feta cheese, all on a delicious crust. The addition of lemon wedges adds a bright and citrusy finish to each bite!

Greek Orzo Salad Pizza

Ingredients:

For the Pizza Dough:

- 1 pound pizza dough (homemade or store-bought)
- Cornmeal or flour for dusting

For the Tzatziki Sauce:

- 1 cup Greek yogurt
- 1/2 cucumber, grated and drained
- 2 cloves garlic, minced
- 1 tablespoon fresh dill, chopped
- 1 tablespoon extra virgin olive oil
- Salt and black pepper to taste

For the Orzo Salad Topping:

- 1 cup cooked orzo pasta, cooled
- 1 cup cherry tomatoes, halved
- 1/2 cup cucumber, diced
- 1/4 cup red onion, finely chopped
- 1/4 cup Kalamata olives, sliced
- 1/4 cup crumbled feta cheese
- 2 tablespoons fresh parsley, chopped
- 1 tablespoon fresh oregano, chopped
- Extra virgin olive oil for drizzling

Instructions:

For the Tzatziki Sauce:

   Prepare the Tzatziki:
   - In a bowl, combine Greek yogurt, grated and drained cucumber, minced garlic, chopped fresh dill, extra virgin olive oil, salt, and black pepper. Mix well.
   - Refrigerate the tzatziki sauce until ready to use.

For the Pizza:

- Preheat the Oven:
    - Preheat your oven to the highest temperature it can go (usually around 475-500°F or 245-260°C).
- Prepare the Dough:
    - Sprinkle cornmeal or flour on a pizza stone or a baking sheet. Place the rolled-out pizza dough on the prepared surface.
- Assemble the Pizza:
    - Spread a generous layer of tzatziki sauce over the pizza dough, leaving a border around the edges for the crust.
    - In a bowl, mix together cooked orzo pasta, halved cherry tomatoes, diced cucumber, finely chopped red onion, sliced Kalamata olives, crumbled feta cheese, fresh chopped parsley, and fresh chopped oregano.
    - Evenly distribute the orzo salad mixture over the tzatziki-covered dough.
- Bake the Pizza:
    - Place the pizza in the preheated oven and bake for 12-15 minutes or until the crust is golden, and the cheese is melted and bubbly.
- Finish and Garnish:
    - Remove the Greek Orzo Salad Pizza from the oven. Drizzle extra virgin olive oil over the top.
- Slice and Serve:
    - Allow the pizza to cool for a few minutes before slicing. Serve and enjoy your flavorful Greek Orzo Salad Pizza!

This pizza combines the freshness of a Greek orzo salad with the creamy goodness of tzatziki sauce, creating a unique and delicious Mediterranean-inspired dish!

Pita Bread Breakfast Pizza with Greek Yogurt

Ingredients:

For the Pita Bread Pizza:

- 4 whole wheat pita bread rounds
- 1 cup cherry tomatoes, halved
- 1/2 cup baby spinach leaves
- 4 large eggs
- 1/2 cup feta cheese, crumbled
- Olive oil for drizzling
- Salt and black pepper to taste

For the Greek Yogurt Topping:

- 1 cup Greek yogurt
- 1 tablespoon fresh dill, chopped
- 1 tablespoon extra virgin olive oil
- Salt and black pepper to taste

Optional Toppings:

- Sliced cucumber
- Kalamata olives, sliced
- Red onion, thinly sliced

Instructions:

For the Greek Yogurt Topping:

Prepare the Greek Yogurt Topping:
- In a bowl, mix together Greek yogurt, chopped fresh dill, extra virgin olive oil, salt, and black pepper. Set aside.

For the Pita Bread Breakfast Pizza:

Preheat the Oven:
- Preheat your oven to 375°F (190°C).

Prepare the Pita Bread:

- Place the whole wheat pita bread rounds on a baking sheet.

Assemble the Pita Bread Pizza:
- Spread a generous layer of the prepared Greek yogurt topping over each pita bread round.
- Evenly distribute cherry tomatoes, baby spinach leaves, and crumbled feta cheese over the Greek yogurt.
- Create a well in the center of each pizza and carefully crack an egg into the well.

Bake the Pita Bread Pizza:
- Place the baking sheet in the preheated oven and bake for 12-15 minutes or until the egg whites are set, and the yolks are still slightly runny.

Optional Toppings:
- If desired, add optional toppings like sliced cucumber, Kalamata olives, and thinly sliced red onion over the baked pizzas.

Finish and Serve:
- Remove the Pita Bread Breakfast Pizzas from the oven. Drizzle olive oil over the top.
- Season with salt and black pepper to taste.
- Serve the breakfast pizzas warm and enjoy!

This Pita Bread Breakfast Pizza with Greek Yogurt offers a nutritious and flavorful start to the day, combining the goodness of eggs, fresh vegetables, and the creaminess of Greek yogurt. Feel free to customize the toppings based on your preferences!

Fennel and Artichoke Greek Pizza

Ingredients:

For the Pizza Dough:

- 1 pound pizza dough (homemade or store-bought)
- Cornmeal or flour for dusting

For the Tomato Sauce:

- 1/2 cup tomato sauce
- 1 tablespoon tomato paste
- 1 clove garlic, minced
- 1 teaspoon dried oregano
- Salt and black pepper to taste

For the Pizza Toppings:

- 1 fennel bulb, thinly sliced
- 1 can (14 ounces) artichoke hearts, drained and sliced
- 1/2 cup Kalamata olives, sliced
- 1/2 cup crumbled feta cheese
- 1/4 cup grated Parmesan cheese
- Fresh dill for garnish
- Extra virgin olive oil for drizzling

Instructions:

For the Tomato Sauce:

Prepare the Tomato Sauce:
- In a bowl, mix together tomato sauce, tomato paste, minced garlic, dried oregano, salt, and black pepper. Set aside.

For the Pizza:

Preheat the Oven:
- Preheat your oven to the highest temperature it can go (usually around 475-500°F or 245-260°C).

Prepare the Dough:
- Sprinkle cornmeal or flour on a pizza stone or a baking sheet. Place the rolled-out pizza dough on the prepared surface.

Assemble the Pizza:
- Spread a layer of the prepared tomato sauce over the pizza dough, leaving a border around the edges for the crust.
- Evenly distribute the thinly sliced fennel, sliced artichoke hearts, and sliced Kalamata olives over the sauce.
- Sprinkle crumbled feta cheese and grated Parmesan cheese over the toppings.

Bake the Pizza:
- Place the pizza in the preheated oven and bake for 12-15 minutes or until the crust is golden, and the cheese is melted and bubbly.

Finish and Garnish:
- Remove the Fennel and Artichoke Greek Pizza from the oven. Sprinkle fresh dill over the hot pizza.
- Drizzle extra virgin olive oil over the pizza.

Slice and Serve:
- Allow the pizza to cool for a few minutes before slicing. Serve and enjoy your flavorful Fennel and Artichoke Greek Pizza!

This pizza showcases the unique combination of flavors from fennel and artichoke, complemented by the brininess of Kalamata olives and the richness of feta cheese. It's a delightful twist on the classic Greek pizza!

Greek-inspired Pita Calzone

Ingredients:

For the Filling:

- 1 cup cooked chicken, shredded (or use rotisserie chicken)
- 1 cup cherry tomatoes, halved
- 1/2 cup cucumber, diced
- 1/4 cup red onion, finely chopped
- 1/4 cup Kalamata olives, sliced
- 1/2 cup crumbled feta cheese
- 1 teaspoon dried oregano
- Salt and black pepper to taste
- Olive oil for drizzling

For the Tzatziki Sauce:

- 1 cup Greek yogurt
- 1/2 cucumber, grated and drained
- 2 cloves garlic, minced
- 1 tablespoon fresh dill, chopped
- 1 tablespoon extra virgin olive oil
- Salt and black pepper to taste

For the Calzone:

- 4 large pita bread rounds
- Olive oil for brushing
- Additional feta cheese for sprinkling (optional)
- Fresh parsley for garnish

Instructions:

For the Tzatziki Sauce:

    Prepare the Tzatziki:

- In a bowl, combine Greek yogurt, grated and drained cucumber, minced garlic, chopped fresh dill, extra virgin olive oil, salt, and black pepper. Mix well.
- Refrigerate the tzatziki sauce until ready to use.

For the Filling:

Prepare the Filling:
- In a bowl, combine shredded cooked chicken, halved cherry tomatoes, diced cucumber, finely chopped red onion, sliced Kalamata olives, crumbled feta cheese, dried oregano, salt, and black pepper. Mix well.

For the Calzone:

Preheat the Oven:
- Preheat your oven to 375°F (190°C).

Prepare the Pita Bread:
- Place the pita bread rounds on a baking sheet.

Assemble the Calzones:
- Spoon the chicken and vegetable filling onto one half of each pita bread round.
- Drizzle a spoonful of tzatziki sauce over the filling.
- Fold the other half of the pita bread over the filling, creating a half-moon shape. Press the edges to seal.

Brush with Olive Oil:
- Brush the tops of the pita calzones with olive oil.

Bake the Calzones:
- Bake in the preheated oven for 15-20 minutes or until the calzones are golden brown and heated through.

Finish and Garnish:
- Remove the Greek-inspired Pita Calzones from the oven. Optionally, sprinkle additional feta cheese over the tops.
- Garnish with fresh parsley.

Serve:
- Serve the calzones warm with extra tzatziki sauce on the side for dipping.

These Greek-inspired Pita Calzones offer a delightful combination of flavors and are perfect for a quick and tasty meal. Enjoy!

Tomato and Olive Pesto Pita Pizza

Ingredients:

For the Pesto:

- 2 cups fresh basil leaves
- 1/2 cup grated Parmesan cheese
- 1/3 cup pine nuts
- 2 cloves garlic, minced
- 1/2 cup extra virgin olive oil
- Salt and black pepper to taste

For the Pita Pizza:

- 4 large whole wheat pita bread rounds
- 1 cup cherry tomatoes, halved
- 1/2 cup Kalamata olives, sliced
- 1/2 cup feta cheese, crumbled
- 1 tablespoon extra virgin olive oil
- Fresh basil leaves for garnish

Instructions:

For the Pesto:

Prepare the Pesto:
- In a food processor, combine fresh basil, grated Parmesan cheese, pine nuts, and minced garlic.
- Pulse until the ingredients are finely chopped.
- With the food processor running, gradually add the olive oil until the pesto reaches a smooth consistency.
- Season with salt and black pepper to taste. Set aside.

For the Pita Pizza:

Preheat the Oven:
- Preheat your oven to 375°F (190°C).

Prepare the Pita Bread:

- Place the pita bread rounds on a baking sheet.

Spread Pesto on Pita:
- Spread a generous amount of the prepared pesto on each pita bread round, leaving a border around the edges.

Add Toppings:
- Arrange halved cherry tomatoes and sliced Kalamata olives over the pesto-covered pita.
- Sprinkle crumbled feta cheese evenly over the toppings.

Drizzle with Olive Oil:
- Drizzle extra virgin olive oil over the top of each pita pizza.

Bake the Pita Pizzas:
- Bake in the preheated oven for 12-15 minutes or until the edges are golden and the toppings are heated through.

Finish and Garnish:
- Remove the Tomato and Olive Pesto Pita Pizzas from the oven.
- Garnish with fresh basil leaves.

Slice and Serve:
- Allow the pita pizzas to cool for a few minutes before slicing. Serve and enjoy your flavorful Tomato and Olive Pesto Pita Pizza!

These pita pizzas are bursting with the fresh and savory flavors of tomatoes, olives, and pesto. They make for a quick and delicious meal or appetizer!

Greek Tandoori Chicken Pizza

Ingredients:

For the Tandoori Chicken:

- 1 pound boneless, skinless chicken breasts, cut into bite-sized pieces
- 1 cup Greek yogurt
- 2 tablespoons tandoori spice blend
- 1 tablespoon lemon juice
- 2 cloves garlic, minced
- 1 teaspoon ginger, grated
- Salt and black pepper to taste

For the Pizza:

- 1 pound pizza dough (homemade or store-bought)
- Cornmeal or flour for dusting
- 1/2 cup tzatziki sauce (store-bought or homemade)
- 1 cup cherry tomatoes, halved
- 1/2 cup red onion, thinly sliced
- 1/2 cup Kalamata olives, sliced
- 1/2 cup feta cheese, crumbled
- Fresh parsley for garnish
- Lemon wedges for serving

Instructions:

For the Tandoori Chicken:

Marinate the Chicken:
- In a bowl, combine Greek yogurt, tandoori spice blend, lemon juice, minced garlic, grated ginger, salt, and black pepper.
- Add the bite-sized chicken pieces to the marinade, ensuring they are well-coated. Cover and refrigerate for at least 2 hours, or overnight for more flavor.

Cook the Chicken:
- Preheat a grill or grill pan over medium-high heat.
- Thread the marinated chicken pieces onto skewers and grill for 8-10 minutes, or until fully cooked and slightly charred.

- Remove the chicken from the skewers and set aside.

For the Pizza:

Preheat the Oven:
- Preheat your oven to the highest temperature it can go (usually around 475-500°F or 245-260°C).

Prepare the Dough:
- Sprinkle cornmeal or flour on a pizza stone or a baking sheet. Place the rolled-out pizza dough on the prepared surface.

Assemble the Pizza:
- Spread a layer of tzatziki sauce over the pizza dough, leaving a border around the edges for the crust.
- Distribute the grilled tandoori chicken evenly over the tzatziki-covered dough.
- Scatter halved cherry tomatoes, thinly sliced red onion, sliced Kalamata olives, and crumbled feta cheese over the pizza.

Bake the Pizza:
- Place the pizza in the preheated oven and bake for 12-15 minutes or until the crust is golden, and the cheese is melted and bubbly.

Finish and Garnish:
- Remove the Greek Tandoori Chicken Pizza from the oven. Sprinkle fresh parsley over the hot pizza.
- Serve with lemon wedges on the side for squeezing over the pizza.

Slice and Serve:
- Allow the pizza to cool for a few minutes before slicing. Serve and enjoy your flavorful Greek Tandoori Chicken Pizza!

This fusion pizza combines the aromatic spices of tandoori chicken with classic Greek toppings, creating a unique and delicious meal. Enjoy the burst of flavors in every bite!

Greek Hummus and Pita Pizza

Ingredients:

For the Hummus:

- 1 can (15 ounces) chickpeas, drained and rinsed
- 1/4 cup tahini
- 2 tablespoons lemon juice
- 2 cloves garlic, minced
- 1/4 cup extra virgin olive oil
- 1/2 teaspoon ground cumin
- Salt and black pepper to taste
- Water (as needed for desired consistency)

For the Pizza:

- 4 whole wheat pita bread rounds
- Olive oil for brushing
- 1 cup cherry tomatoes, halved
- 1/2 cup cucumber, diced
- 1/4 cup red onion, thinly sliced
- 1/4 cup Kalamata olives, sliced
- 1/2 cup crumbled feta cheese
- Fresh oregano or parsley for garnish

Instructions:

For the Hummus:

Prepare the Hummus:
- In a food processor, combine chickpeas, tahini, lemon juice, minced garlic, extra virgin olive oil, ground cumin, salt, and black pepper.
- Blend until smooth, adding water as needed to achieve your desired consistency.
- Taste and adjust seasonings, if necessary. Set aside.

For the Pizza:

Preheat the Oven:

- Preheat your oven to 375°F (190°C).

Prepare the Pita Bread:
- Place the whole wheat pita bread rounds on a baking sheet.

Brush with Olive Oil:
- Lightly brush the tops of each pita bread with olive oil.

Spread Hummus on Pita:
- Spread a generous layer of the prepared hummus over each pita bread, covering the entire surface.

Add Toppings:
- Arrange halved cherry tomatoes, diced cucumber, thinly sliced red onion, sliced Kalamata olives, and crumbled feta cheese over the hummus-covered pita bread.

Bake the Pita Pizzas:
- Bake in the preheated oven for 12-15 minutes or until the edges are golden, and the toppings are heated through.

Finish and Garnish:
- Remove the Greek Hummus and Pita Pizzas from the oven.
- Garnish with fresh oregano or parsley.

Slice and Serve:
- Allow the pizzas to cool for a few minutes before slicing. Serve and enjoy your flavorful Greek Hummus and Pita Pizza!

This pizza offers a healthy and delicious twist with the creamy hummus base and the vibrant Greek-inspired toppings. It's a perfect option for a quick and satisfying meal!

Mediterranean Roasted Vegetable Flatbread Pizza

Ingredients:

For the Roasted Vegetables:

- 1 zucchini, sliced
- 1 red bell pepper, sliced
- 1 yellow bell pepper, sliced
- 1 red onion, thinly sliced
- 1 cup cherry tomatoes, halved
- 2 tablespoons olive oil
- 1 teaspoon dried oregano
- Salt and black pepper to taste

For the Flatbread Pizza:

- 4 whole wheat or regular flatbreads
- 1/2 cup hummus (store-bought or homemade)
- 1/2 cup crumbled feta cheese
- 1/4 cup Kalamata olives, sliced
- Fresh parsley, chopped, for garnish
- Lemon wedges for serving

Instructions:

For the Roasted Vegetables:

Preheat the Oven:
- Preheat your oven to 425°F (220°C).

Prepare the Vegetables:
- In a large bowl, toss together sliced zucchini, red bell pepper, yellow bell pepper, red onion, and halved cherry tomatoes.

Season and Roast:
- Drizzle olive oil over the vegetables and sprinkle with dried oregano, salt, and black pepper. Toss to coat evenly.
- Spread the vegetables on a baking sheet in a single layer.

- Roast in the preheated oven for 20-25 minutes or until the vegetables are tender and slightly caramelized, stirring halfway through.

For the Flatbread Pizza:

Prepare the Flatbreads:
- Place the flatbreads on a baking sheet.

Spread Hummus:
- Spread a layer of hummus over each flatbread, leaving a border around the edges.

Add Roasted Vegetables:
- Distribute the roasted vegetables evenly over the hummus-covered flatbreads.

Sprinkle Feta Cheese:
- Sprinkle crumbled feta cheese over the vegetables.

Add Kalamata Olives:
- Scatter sliced Kalamata olives over the flatbreads.

Bake the Pizzas:
- Bake in the preheated oven for 10-12 minutes or until the edges of the flatbreads are crispy and the toppings are heated through.

Finish and Garnish:
- Remove the Mediterranean Roasted Vegetable Flatbread Pizzas from the oven.
- Garnish with chopped fresh parsley.

Serve with Lemon Wedges:
- Serve the flatbread pizzas with lemon wedges on the side for squeezing over the pizza.

Slice and Enjoy:
- Allow the pizzas to cool for a few minutes before slicing. Serve and enjoy your flavorful Mediterranean Roasted Vegetable Flatbread Pizza!

This pizza celebrates the vibrant flavors of the Mediterranean with a combination of roasted vegetables, hummus, feta cheese, and olives on a crispy flatbread. It's a delightful and wholesome meal!

Greek Potato and Rosemary Pizza

Ingredients:

For the Pizza Dough:

- 1 pound pizza dough (homemade or store-bought)
- Cornmeal or flour for dusting

For the Potato Topping:

- 2 medium-sized potatoes, thinly sliced
- 2 tablespoons olive oil
- 1 tablespoon fresh rosemary, chopped
- Salt and black pepper to taste

For the Pizza:

- 1/2 cup tzatziki sauce (store-bought or homemade)
- 1 cup feta cheese, crumbled
- 1/2 cup Kalamata olives, sliced
- 1/4 cup red onion, thinly sliced
- Olive oil for drizzling
- Fresh rosemary for garnish

Instructions:

For the Potato Topping:

Preheat the Oven:
- Preheat your oven to 400°F (200°C).

Prepare the Potatoes:
- In a bowl, toss thinly sliced potatoes with olive oil, chopped fresh rosemary, salt, and black pepper.

Roast the Potatoes:
- Spread the seasoned potato slices on a baking sheet in a single layer.

- Roast in the preheated oven for 15-20 minutes or until the potatoes are tender and slightly crispy.
- Remove from the oven and set aside.

For the Pizza:

Preheat the Oven:
- Preheat your oven to the highest temperature it can go (usually around 475-500°F or 245-260°C).

Prepare the Dough:
- Sprinkle cornmeal or flour on a pizza stone or a baking sheet. Place the rolled-out pizza dough on the prepared surface.

Spread Tzatziki:
- Spread a layer of tzatziki sauce over the pizza dough, leaving a border around the edges for the crust.

Add Potatoes and Toppings:
- Arrange the roasted potato slices over the tzatziki-covered dough.
- Sprinkle crumbled feta cheese over the potatoes.
- Scatter sliced Kalamata olives and thinly sliced red onion over the pizza.

Drizzle with Olive Oil:
- Drizzle olive oil over the top of the pizza.

Bake the Pizza:
- Place the pizza in the preheated oven and bake for 12-15 minutes or until the crust is golden, and the cheese is melted and bubbly.

Finish and Garnish:
- Remove the Greek Potato and Rosemary Pizza from the oven. Sprinkle fresh rosemary over the hot pizza.

Slice and Serve:
- Allow the pizza to cool for a few minutes before slicing. Serve and enjoy your flavorful Greek Potato and Rosemary Pizza!

This pizza combines the earthy flavors of roasted potatoes and rosemary with the classic Greek toppings, creating a unique and delicious Mediterranean-inspired dish. Enjoy!

Smoked Salmon and Cream Cheese Greek Pizza

Ingredients:

For the Pizza Dough:

- 1 pound pizza dough (homemade or store-bought)
- Cornmeal or flour for dusting

For the Cream Cheese Spread:

- 1/2 cup cream cheese, softened
- 2 tablespoons fresh dill, chopped
- 1 tablespoon lemon juice
- Salt and black pepper to taste

For the Pizza:

- 1/2 cup tzatziki sauce (store-bought or homemade)
- 4 ounces smoked salmon, thinly sliced
- 1/4 cup red onion, thinly sliced
- 1/4 cup cucumber, thinly sliced
- 2 tablespoons capers
- Fresh dill for garnish
- Lemon wedges for serving

Instructions:

For the Cream Cheese Spread:

Prepare the Cream Cheese Spread:
- In a bowl, combine softened cream cheese, chopped fresh dill, lemon juice, salt, and black pepper. Mix well.

For the Pizza:

Preheat the Oven:
- Preheat your oven to the highest temperature it can go (usually around 475-500°F or 245-260°C).

Prepare the Dough:

- Sprinkle cornmeal or flour on a pizza stone or a baking sheet. Place the rolled-out pizza dough on the prepared surface.

Spread Tzatziki:
- Spread a layer of tzatziki sauce over the pizza dough, leaving a border around the edges for the crust.

Add Cream Cheese Spread:
- Spoon dollops of the cream cheese spread over the tzatziki-covered dough.

Layer with Smoked Salmon and Toppings:
- Arrange the thinly sliced smoked salmon over the cream cheese and tzatziki.
- Scatter thinly sliced red onion and cucumber over the pizza.
- Sprinkle capers evenly over the toppings.

Bake the Pizza:
- Place the pizza in the preheated oven and bake for 12-15 minutes or until the crust is golden, and the toppings are heated through.

Finish and Garnish:
- Remove the Smoked Salmon and Cream Cheese Greek Pizza from the oven. Garnish with fresh dill.

Serve with Lemon Wedges:
- Serve the pizza slices with lemon wedges on the side for squeezing over the smoked salmon.

Slice and Enjoy:
- Allow the pizza to cool for a few minutes before slicing. Serve and enjoy your flavorful Smoked Salmon and Cream Cheese Greek Pizza!

This pizza combines the luxurious taste of smoked salmon with creamy cream cheese and classic Greek flavors for a delicious and elegant twist. Enjoy!

Spinach and Olive Greek Pizza Breadsticks

Ingredients:

For the Pizza Dough:

- 1 pound pizza dough (homemade or store-bought)
- Cornmeal or flour for dusting

For the Spinach and Olive Topping:

- 2 cups fresh spinach, chopped
- 1/2 cup Kalamata olives, sliced
- 1/4 cup red onion, finely chopped
- 1 cup feta cheese, crumbled
- 1 tablespoon olive oil
- 1 teaspoon dried oregano
- Salt and black pepper to taste

For the Garlic Herb Butter:

- 1/2 cup unsalted butter, melted
- 3 cloves garlic, minced
- 1 teaspoon dried oregano
- 1 teaspoon dried basil
- 1/2 teaspoon dried thyme
- 1/2 teaspoon dried rosemary

For the Tzatziki Dip:

- 1 cup Greek yogurt
- 1/2 cucumber, grated and drained
- 2 cloves garlic, minced
- 1 tablespoon fresh dill, chopped
- 1 tablespoon extra virgin olive oil
- Salt and black pepper to taste

Instructions:

For the Spinach and Olive Topping:

Prepare the Topping:
- In a bowl, combine chopped fresh spinach, sliced Kalamata olives, finely chopped red onion, crumbled feta cheese, olive oil, dried oregano, salt, and black pepper. Mix well.

For the Garlic Herb Butter:

Prepare the Garlic Herb Butter:
- In a small saucepan, melt the unsalted butter over low heat.
- Add minced garlic, dried oregano, dried basil, dried thyme, and dried rosemary to the melted butter. Stir until the garlic is fragrant.

For the Pizza Breadsticks:

Preheat the Oven:
- Preheat your oven to 400°F (200°C).

Prepare the Dough:
- Sprinkle cornmeal or flour on a baking sheet.
- Roll out the pizza dough into a rectangular shape on the prepared baking sheet.

Add the Spinach and Olive Topping:
- Spread the prepared spinach and olive topping evenly over the rolled-out pizza dough.

Roll the Dough:
- Starting from one edge, carefully roll the dough to form a log or cylinder.

Slice into Breadsticks:
- Using a sharp knife, slice the rolled dough into 1-inch thick rounds, creating individual breadsticks.

Brush with Garlic Herb Butter:
- Brush the tops of each breadstick with the prepared garlic herb butter.

Bake the Breadsticks:
- Bake in the preheated oven for 15-20 minutes or until the breadsticks are golden brown and cooked through.

For the Tzatziki Dip:

- Prepare the Tzatziki Dip:
  - In a bowl, combine Greek yogurt, grated and drained cucumber, minced garlic, chopped fresh dill, extra virgin olive oil, salt, and black pepper. Mix well.
- Serve and Enjoy:
  - Serve the Spinach and Olive Greek Pizza Breadsticks warm with the tzatziki dip on the side.

These pizza breadsticks combine the flavors of Greek spinach and olive pizza with a delicious garlic herb butter for a tasty and satisfying treat. Enjoy!

Greek Fava Bean and Mint Pizza

Ingredients:

For the Pizza Dough:

- 1 pound pizza dough (homemade or store-bought)
- Cornmeal or flour for dusting

For the Fava Bean and Mint Topping:

- 1 cup cooked fava beans (or canned fava beans, drained)
- 2 tablespoons extra virgin olive oil
- 2 cloves garlic, minced
- 1 tablespoon fresh mint, chopped
- Zest of 1 lemon
- Salt and black pepper to taste

For the Pizza:

- 1/2 cup crumbled feta cheese
- 1/4 cup Kalamata olives, sliced
- 1/4 cup red onion, thinly sliced
- Olive oil for drizzling
- Fresh mint leaves for garnish
- Lemon wedges for serving

Instructions:

For the Fava Bean and Mint Topping:

Prepare the Fava Beans:
- If using fresh fava beans, cook them according to package instructions. If using canned fava beans, drain and rinse them.

Sauté with Garlic and Mint:
- In a skillet, heat 2 tablespoons of extra virgin olive oil over medium heat.
- Add minced garlic and sauté for 1-2 minutes until fragrant.

- Add the cooked fava beans to the skillet, stirring to coat them in the garlic-infused oil.
- Stir in chopped fresh mint, lemon zest, salt, and black pepper. Cook for an additional 2-3 minutes.

Remove from Heat:
- Remove the fava bean and mint mixture from the heat and set aside.

For the Pizza:

Preheat the Oven:
- Preheat your oven to the highest temperature it can go (usually around 475-500°F or 245-260°C).

Prepare the Dough:
- Sprinkle cornmeal or flour on a pizza stone or a baking sheet. Place the rolled-out pizza dough on the prepared surface.

Spread Fava Bean and Mint Mixture:
- Spread the prepared fava bean and mint mixture evenly over the pizza dough, leaving a border around the edges for the crust.

Add Feta, Olives, and Onion:
- Sprinkle crumbled feta cheese over the fava bean mixture.
- Scatter sliced Kalamata olives and thinly sliced red onion over the pizza.

Drizzle with Olive Oil:
- Drizzle olive oil over the top of the pizza.

Bake the Pizza:
- Place the pizza in the preheated oven and bake for 12-15 minutes or until the crust is golden, and the toppings are heated through.

Finish and Garnish:
- Remove the Greek Fava Bean and Mint Pizza from the oven. Garnish with fresh mint leaves.

Serve with Lemon Wedges:
- Serve the pizza slices with lemon wedges on the side for squeezing over the pizza.

Slice and Enjoy:
- Allow the pizza to cool for a few minutes before slicing. Serve and enjoy your unique and flavorful Greek Fava Bean and Mint Pizza!

This pizza offers a fresh and vibrant twist with the combination of fava beans, mint, and lemon, creating a delightful Greek-inspired dish. Enjoy!

Greek Avocado and Tomato Pizza

Ingredients:

For the Pizza Dough:

- 1 pound pizza dough (homemade or store-bought)
- Cornmeal or flour for dusting

For the Avocado and Tomato Topping:

- 2 ripe avocados, sliced
- 1 cup cherry tomatoes, halved
- 1/4 cup red onion, thinly sliced
- 1/4 cup Kalamata olives, sliced
- 1/2 cup crumbled feta cheese
- 2 tablespoons extra virgin olive oil
- 1 tablespoon fresh lemon juice
- Salt and black pepper to taste
- Fresh oregano or basil for garnish

For the Tzatziki Drizzle:

- 1/2 cup Greek yogurt
- 1/2 cucumber, grated and drained
- 2 cloves garlic, minced
- 1 tablespoon fresh dill, chopped
- 1 tablespoon extra virgin olive oil
- Salt and black pepper to taste

Instructions:

For the Avocado and Tomato Topping:

  Prepare the Avocados:
  - Slice the avocados and drizzle them with fresh lemon juice to prevent browning.

  Assemble the Toppings:

- In a bowl, combine halved cherry tomatoes, thinly sliced red onion, sliced Kalamata olives, crumbled feta cheese, extra virgin olive oil, salt, and black pepper. Toss gently to mix.

For the Tzatziki Drizzle:

Prepare the Tzatziki Drizzle:
- In a bowl, combine Greek yogurt, grated and drained cucumber, minced garlic, chopped fresh dill, extra virgin olive oil, salt, and black pepper. Mix well.

For the Pizza:

Preheat the Oven:
- Preheat your oven to the highest temperature it can go (usually around 475-500°F or 245-260°C).

Prepare the Dough:
- Sprinkle cornmeal or flour on a pizza stone or a baking sheet. Place the rolled-out pizza dough on the prepared surface.

Assemble the Pizza:
- Spread the avocado slices over the pizza dough, leaving a border around the edges for the crust.
- Spoon the prepared tomato and olive mixture evenly over the avocado-covered dough.

Bake the Pizza:
- Place the pizza in the preheated oven and bake for 12-15 minutes or until the crust is golden, and the toppings are heated through.

Finish and Garnish:
- Remove the Greek Avocado and Tomato Pizza from the oven. Garnish with fresh oregano or basil.

Drizzle with Tzatziki:
- Drizzle the tzatziki sauce over the hot pizza.

Slice and Serve:
- Allow the pizza to cool for a few minutes before slicing. Serve and enjoy your fresh and flavorful Greek Avocado and Tomato Pizza!

This pizza offers a refreshing twist with creamy avocado, juicy tomatoes, and a tangy tzatziki drizzle, creating a delightful Mediterranean-inspired dish. Enjoy!

Mediterranean Quiche Pizza

Ingredients:

For the Pizza Dough:

- 1 pound pizza dough (homemade or store-bought)
- Cornmeal or flour for dusting

For the Quiche Filling:

- 4 large eggs
- 1 cup milk
- 1/2 cup feta cheese, crumbled
- 1/2 cup cherry tomatoes, halved
- 1/4 cup Kalamata olives, sliced
- 1/4 cup red onion, finely chopped
- 1/4 cup spinach, chopped
- 1 teaspoon dried oregano
- Salt and black pepper to taste

For the Topping:

- 1/2 cup mozzarella cheese, shredded
- 2 tablespoons fresh parsley, chopped
- Olive oil for drizzling

Instructions:

For the Quiche Filling:

Prepare the Quiche Filling:
- In a bowl, whisk together eggs and milk until well combined.
- Stir in crumbled feta cheese, halved cherry tomatoes, sliced Kalamata olives, finely chopped red onion, chopped spinach, dried oregano, salt, and black pepper.

For the Pizza:

Preheat the Oven:

- Preheat your oven to 375°F (190°C).

Prepare the Dough:
- Sprinkle cornmeal or flour on a pizza stone or a baking sheet. Place the rolled-out pizza dough on the prepared surface.

Assemble the Pizza:
- Pour the quiche filling over the rolled-out pizza dough, spreading it evenly.

Add Toppings:
- Sprinkle shredded mozzarella cheese over the quiche filling.
- Drizzle olive oil over the top.

Bake the Pizza:
- Place the pizza in the preheated oven and bake for 20-25 minutes or until the crust is golden, and the quiche filling is set.

Finish and Garnish:
- Remove the Mediterranean Quiche Pizza from the oven. Sprinkle chopped fresh parsley over the hot pizza.

Slice and Serve:
- Allow the pizza to cool for a few minutes before slicing. Serve and enjoy your unique Mediterranean Quiche Pizza!

This recipe combines the flavors of a classic quiche with the convenience of a pizza, offering a delightful twist on both dishes. Enjoy the creamy texture of the quiche filling and the Mediterranean-inspired toppings!

Greek Feta and Honey Pizza

Ingredients:

For the Pizza Dough:

- 1 pound pizza dough (homemade or store-bought)
- Cornmeal or flour for dusting

For the Topping:

- 1 cup crumbled feta cheese
- 1/4 cup Kalamata olives, sliced
- 1/4 cup cherry tomatoes, halved
- 2 tablespoons red onion, thinly sliced
- 2 tablespoons fresh oregano, chopped
- 2 tablespoons extra virgin olive oil
- Salt and black pepper to taste

For the Honey Drizzle:

- 2 tablespoons honey

Optional Garnish:

- Fresh mint leaves

Instructions:

For the Pizza:

> Preheat the Oven:
> - Preheat your oven to the highest temperature it can go (usually around 475-500°F or 245-260°C).
>
> Prepare the Dough:
> - Sprinkle cornmeal or flour on a pizza stone or a baking sheet. Place the rolled-out pizza dough on the prepared surface.
>
> Assemble the Pizza:
> - Spread crumbled feta cheese evenly over the rolled-out pizza dough, leaving a border around the edges for the crust.

- Scatter sliced Kalamata olives, halved cherry tomatoes, and thinly sliced red onion over the feta cheese.

Sprinkle with Oregano:
- Sprinkle chopped fresh oregano over the pizza toppings.

Drizzle with Olive Oil:
- Drizzle extra virgin olive oil over the top of the pizza.

Season with Salt and Pepper:
- Season the pizza with salt and black pepper to taste.

Bake the Pizza:
- Place the pizza in the preheated oven and bake for 12-15 minutes or until the crust is golden, and the toppings are heated through.

For the Honey Drizzle:

Drizzle with Honey:
- Remove the Greek Feta and Honey Pizza from the oven. Drizzle honey over the hot pizza.

Optional Garnish:

Garnish with Fresh Mint:
- Garnish the pizza with fresh mint leaves for added freshness and flavor.

Slice and Serve:
- Allow the pizza to cool for a few minutes before slicing. Serve and enjoy your delicious Greek Feta and Honey Pizza!

This pizza combines the creamy and salty flavor of feta with the sweetness of honey, creating a delightful Mediterranean-inspired dish. The addition of Kalamata olives, cherry tomatoes, and fresh oregano adds extra layers of flavor. Enjoy!

Kalamata Olive and Rosemary Focaccia Pizza

Ingredients:

For the Focaccia Dough:

- 1 pound focaccia dough (homemade or store-bought)
- Olive oil for drizzling
- Coarse sea salt for sprinkling

For the Topping:

- 1/2 cup Kalamata olives, pitted and sliced
- 2 tablespoons fresh rosemary, chopped
- 1/4 cup red onion, thinly sliced
- 1 cup mozzarella cheese, shredded
- 2 tablespoons Parmesan cheese, grated

Optional Garnish:

- Fresh arugula

Instructions:

For the Focaccia Dough:

  Prepare the Focaccia Dough:
  - If using store-bought dough, follow the package instructions. If making homemade focaccia dough, let it rise according to the recipe instructions.

  Preheat the Oven:
  - Preheat your oven to 425°F (220°C).

  Shape the Focaccia:
  - Roll out the focaccia dough onto a baking sheet, shaping it into a rectangle or your desired pizza shape.

  Drizzle with Olive Oil:
  - Drizzle olive oil over the surface of the focaccia dough.

  Sprinkle with Sea Salt:
  - Sprinkle coarse sea salt over the oiled dough for added flavor.

For the Topping:

Add Kalamata Olives and Rosemary:
- Distribute sliced Kalamata olives and chopped fresh rosemary evenly over the focaccia dough.

Add Red Onion:
- Scatter thinly sliced red onion over the olives and rosemary.

Sprinkle with Cheeses:
- Sprinkle shredded mozzarella cheese and grated Parmesan cheese over the toppings.

Bake the Focaccia Pizza:
- Place the focaccia pizza in the preheated oven and bake for 15-20 minutes or until the crust is golden and the cheese is melted and bubbly.

Optional Garnish:

Top with Fresh Arugula:
- Remove the focaccia pizza from the oven. If desired, top with a handful of fresh arugula for a peppery kick and added freshness.

Slice and Serve:
- Allow the Kalamata Olive and Rosemary Focaccia Pizza to cool for a few minutes before slicing. Serve and enjoy!

This focaccia pizza offers a delightful combination of briny Kalamata olives, aromatic rosemary, and the cheesy goodness of mozzarella and Parmesan. The addition of fresh arugula on top adds a burst of color and flavor. Enjoy your homemade pizza!

Grilled Greek Pizza Panini

Ingredients:

For the Pizza Panini:

- 1 pound pizza dough (homemade or store-bought)
- Olive oil for brushing
- 1 cup mozzarella cheese, shredded
- 1/2 cup feta cheese, crumbled
- 1/4 cup Kalamata olives, sliced
- 1/4 cup sun-dried tomatoes, chopped
- 1/4 cup red onion, thinly sliced
- 1/2 teaspoon dried oregano
- Salt and black pepper to taste

For the Tzatziki Sauce:

- 1/2 cup Greek yogurt
- 1/2 cucumber, grated and drained
- 2 cloves garlic, minced
- 1 tablespoon fresh dill, chopped
- 1 tablespoon extra virgin olive oil
- Salt and black pepper to taste

Optional Additions:

- Fresh spinach leaves
- Sliced bell peppers
- Sliced tomatoes

Instructions:

For the Tzatziki Sauce:

    Prepare the Tzatziki Sauce:
- In a bowl, combine Greek yogurt, grated and drained cucumber, minced garlic, chopped fresh dill, extra virgin olive oil, salt, and black pepper. Mix well. Set aside.

For the Pizza Panini:

Preheat the Grill or Panini Press:
- Preheat your grill or panini press.

Prepare the Pizza Dough:
- Roll out the pizza dough into a rectangle or your desired shape.

Brush with Olive Oil:
- Brush one side of the pizza dough with olive oil.

Assemble the Panini:
- Place the oiled side of the dough facing down on the grill or panini press.
- On one half of the dough, layer mozzarella cheese, crumbled feta, sliced Kalamata olives, chopped sun-dried tomatoes, thinly sliced red onion, dried oregano, salt, and black pepper. Optionally, add fresh spinach leaves, sliced bell peppers, or sliced tomatoes.
- Fold the other half of the dough over the toppings, creating a sandwich.

Grill the Panini:
- Grill the pizza panini for 3-5 minutes on each side, or until the crust is golden and the cheese is melted.

Remove and Slice:
- Carefully remove the grilled Greek pizza panini from the grill or panini press.
- Slice the panini into smaller portions.

Serve with Tzatziki Sauce:
- Serve the grilled Greek pizza panini with a side of the prepared tzatziki sauce for dipping.

Enjoy:
- Enjoy your Grilled Greek Pizza Panini with the delicious flavors of Mediterranean ingredients and the creamy goodness of tzatziki sauce!

This grilled pizza panini is a perfect blend of Greek flavors, and the addition of homemade tzatziki sauce adds a refreshing touch. Customize the toppings to suit your preferences and savor the delightful combination of melted cheeses and Mediterranean goodness.